Table of Contents

Pot holders are useful and make perfect gifts. They can be made from fabric scraps and bits of leftover batting. The patterns given here may be made into pot holders or used to make blocks for quilts. Whether you make small pot holders or large quilts, you will enjoy the variety of patterns given.

Sparkling Stars 4
Beautiful Baskets 9
Garden of Flowers 16
Patriotic Mosaics 24

Chocolate Confections 30
Culinary Delights 37
Melon Patch 42
Italian Flavors 50
Homey Comforts 52
Summer Sunshine 58
Tangy Treats 62
Hot & Sassy 66
Classic Cuisine 70
Baking Pleasure 74
Berry Burst 78
Appliqué General Instructions 82
Lucky Shamrock 83
Spring Tulips 84
Apples & Cherries 86
Fall Harvest 88
Framed Poinsettia 91
Dresden Place Poinsettia 92
Candles & Holly 94

General Instructions

Basic Instructions

The instructions that follow apply to all the patterns given. These patterns may be used to make matching wall hangings, place mats or table runners. Be creative in your fabric choices and make up dozens of these for yourself or your family and friends.

Color suggestions are given with each pot holder to correspond to colors used in the samples. These are suggestions to show you placement of background and contrasting pieces that form the design when stitched.

Project Notes

Scraps of leftover fabrics from other projects are perfect choices to use when making pot holders. If you prefer to purchase fabrics for a planned color scheme, a fat quarter (piece of fabric cut 18" x 22") of each of four fabrics would be enough to make several pot holders. Some fibers are very flammable, and since pot holders are held near flames or heat, they should be flame-resistant; we recommend 100 percent cotton fabrics be used for the pieced top sections. The backing could be made of a nonflammable fabric especially made for this purpose.

There are several ways to finish the edges of the pot holders. Purchased or self-made bias tapes, rickrack or cording may be used. These should match the fabrics used for the patchwork piecing.

Pot holders must be thick enough to keep the heat from the hot item from penetrating to your hands. Several layers of an inflammable cotton batting or fleece will work, but it should be dense and thick. If you want to use scraps of leftover batting, test the project using a varying number of layers until you have the right number of layers to prevent burning.

Fabrics may be prewashed before using, but it is not necessary. Fabrics should be colorfast, as pot holders do get wet and require frequent washings.

Use all-purpose sewing thread for all piecing. It may also be used for machine-quilting. Nylon monofilament thread may be used for machine-quilting; however, when exposed to flames, it will melt.

Pot holders may be embellished with buttons, laces and trims. Unless it will be used purely as a decorative item, these embellishments should not hamper the usefulness of the pot holder. Buttons sewn in the center of a pot holder would not make it easy to hold a pan.

Template plastic or cardboard may be used to make sturdy patterns. If using cardboard, you might want to copy the patterns given in this pattern book onto paper by tracing or using a copy machine. *Note: Check the copies with the original to be sure they are accurate; some copy machines do not copy actual size.*

To make patterns on cardboard, cut out the paper patterns on the solid line and glue to cardboard and cut out. If using template plastic, place the plastic over the paper patterns and trace onto plastic; cut out.

Tools

To machine-piece the blocks, you will need a well-tuned sewing machine and a new all-purpose needle.

Sharp scissors are needed for trimming and shears for cutting fabric patches. A steam iron is needed for pressing finished blocks.

If you use quick-cutting and -piecing methods without templates, you will need a rotary cutter, plastic ruler and self-healing mat. Measure the templates needed for the chosen design. If you will be using squares, simply cut squares the size of the templates.

To make triangles, cut squares on the diagonal. Measure one of the short sides of the triangle template needed and cut a square that size. Cut the square on the diagonal to make two triangles.

These methods save time when cutting many pieces of the same fabrics for a quilt. The time saved making one block is minimal, and quick methods might not be much faster than cutting templates the traditional way.

How to Use the Patterns

To piece a block, refer to the color drawing of each design. A piecing diagram showing unit-piecing suggestions and a list of the templates needed are given for each design. Note that several sets of patterns share the same templates. Once you have made permanent templates for the pattern pieces, they can be used over and over again to make many other designs.

A ¼" seam allowance has been added to each piece to make machine-piecing easy. If you prefer to hand-piece the blocks, make templates eliminating the seam allowance when tracing. Appliqué pieces require a ¼" seam allowance be added when cutting fabric from templates given without seam allowance.

Place the template on the wrong side of the fabric; trace around outside edge with a pencil or other permanent marker. Cut out pieces on the traced lines for machine-piecing. For hand-piecing, add the ¼" seam allowance when cutting. Cut as directed with each pattern to complete the chosen design.

Making Pot Holders From Blocks

When the block is complete, borders may be added if desired. Press seams toward strips if borders are added. Cut batting and backing pieces 2" larger all around than the pot holder.

The pot holder may be finished in a number of methods. One method is to lay the finished block right sides together with the backing. Place batting piece on top. Cut a piece of bias binding 3" long (or longer) for hanging loop, if desired. Sew along open edges of binding to close. Fold the binding loop in half and place at a corner between the pieced block and the backing with loop to the inside.

Sew a ¼" seam all around outside edges, leaving a 3"–4" opening. Trim corners; turn right side out through opening and press. Slipstitch opening closed by hand to finish.

Piping may be added to the edges before sewing the layers together. Measure distance around pot holder edges; cut a piece of piping this length plus 3". Pin to pieced block as shown in Figure 1. Sew all around, overlapping at the beginning and end; trim excess. Finish pot holder using method given for unbound edges to complete.

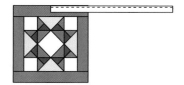

Figure 1
Pin piping to pieced block
as shown.

A second method is to bind the edges with either self-made or purchased binding. To make self-made binding, cut a 1½" x 30" strip (for 6" pot holders) or 1½" x 54" (for 12" pot holders) of coordinating fabric. Fold each long edge ¼" to wrong side; fold strip in half lengthwise with wrong sides together as shown in Figure 2; press.

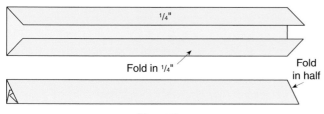

Figure 2
Prepare binding from 1½" fabric strips as shown.

Unfold strip and place short ends right sides together; stitch across ends with ¼" seam allowance. Turn folded edges back in and press. Place binding over raw edge of pieced block, sandwiching block between folded edges of binding. Begin sewing at one corner referring to Figure 3. Stitch along inner edge of binding, making sure to sew both the top and bottom binding seam at the same time to eliminate hand-stitching the binding to the back later.

Figure 3
Sew binding around edges and
make loop as shown.

Continue around each side, either mitering or rounding corners as shown in Figure 4. When you have reached the starting point, you will have some binding left for the loop. Overlap beginning point and continue stitching on edge of binding to finish loop. Stop stitching at beginning point.

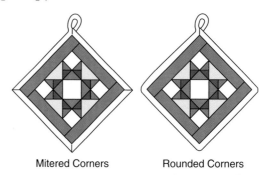

Mitered Corners   Rounded Corners

Figure 4
Sew binding to edges, mitering or
rounding corners as shown.

If you prefer, the binding may be stitched to the pot holder on only one side then turned to the back and hand-stitched in place to finish.

A purchased plastic ring may be substituted for the bias loop for hanging: Cut and fold bias strip as described for bias-loop hanger. Do not sew ends together. Place end of strip over edge of pieced block, sandwiching as previously described, at center of one side of block. Sew all around as for bias loop hanger; just before reaching beginning edge of binding, measure ⅛" plus enough of strip to overlap. Cut off excess and fold end of strip under ⅛". Finish stitching binding. See Figure 5. Sew the ring to the backside of the finished pot holder with matching thread to secure. ■

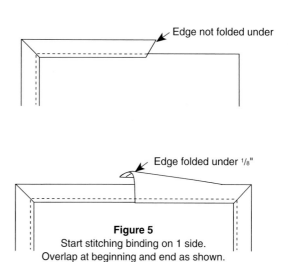

Figure 5
Start stitching binding on 1 side.
Overlap at beginning and end as shown.

Sparkling Stars

Brighten your kitchen with these striking star designs.

Block Size
7" x 8"

Fabric
Scraps of the following fabrics: floral, green, yellow, rose
6 strips 1½" x 8" border fabric

Instructions

Morning Star

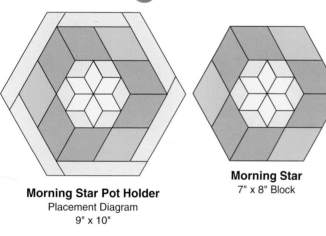

Morning Star Pot Holder
Placement Diagram
9" x 10"

Morning Star
7" x 8" Block

1. Prepare templates using pattern pieces given. Cut as directed on each piece. Template A is on page 6.

2. To piece block, join six yellow center B diamonds to make star design, sewing only to the end of the marked seam lines. Sew in six floral B pieces all around star design. Sew one rose A to the pieced unit as shown in Figure 1.

3. Sew a rose A and a green A together as shown in Figure 2; repeat for three A-A units. Sew one unit to the adjacent side of the previously stitched

A on the B-B unit as shown in Figure 3.

4. Continue adding the A-A units in a clockwise direction referring to the block drawing for color placement.

5. Sew a border strip to one side of the pieced block; press seams toward strip and trim excess as shown in Figure 4. Continue adding strips in a clockwise direction, pressing and trimming after each addition.

6. Finish pot holder as in General Instructions.

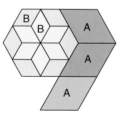

Figure 1
Sew a rose A to the B-B unit.

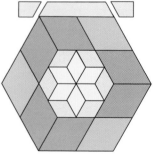

Figure 2
Sew a rose A to a green A.

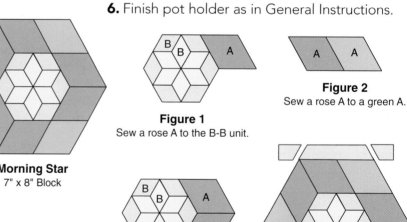

Figure 3
Sew the A-A unit to the pieced unit.

Figure 4
Trim excess strip as shown.

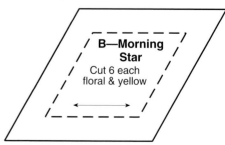

B—Morning Star
Cut 6 each
floral & yellow

Favorite Star

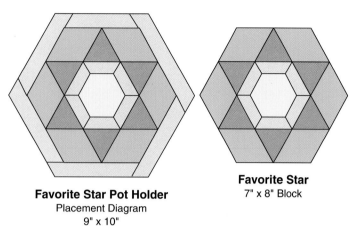

Favorite Star Pot Holder
Placement Diagram
9" x 10"

Favorite Star
7" x 8" Block

3. Sew A to B to A as shown in Figure 2; repeat for three units. Sew one of these units to each side of the C-D unit to complete one block as shown in Figure 3.

4. Sew a border strip to one side of the pieced block; press seams toward strip and trim excess as shown in Figure 4. Continue adding strips in a clockwise direction, pressing and trimming after each addition.

1. Prepare templates using pattern pieces given. Cut as directed on each piece.

2. To piece block, sew all C pieces to D. Sew a B triangle to every other C piece as shown in Figure 1.

5. Finish pot holder as in General Instructions.

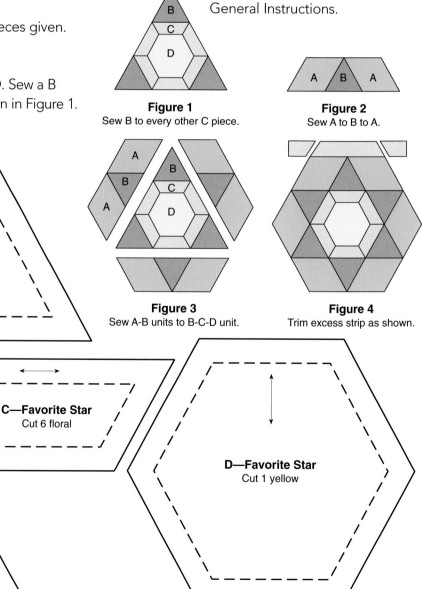

Figure 1
Sew B to every other C piece.

Figure 2
Sew A to B to A.

Figure 3
Sew A-B units to B-C-D unit.

Figure 4
Trim excess strip as shown.

A—Favorite Star
Cut 6 green

A—Morning Star
Cut 3 green & 6 rose

C—Favorite Star
Cut 6 floral

D—Favorite Star
Cut 1 yellow

B—Favorite Star
Cut 6 rose

Outreach Star

1. Prepare templates using pattern pieces given. Cut as directed on each piece.

2. To piece block, join six B pieces as shown in Figure 1, stopping stitching at marked seam lines.

3. Sew A pieces in between B points as shown in Figure 2.

4. Turn under seam allowance on C; center and appliqué over B centers to complete one block as shown in Figure 3.

5. Sew border strip to one side of the pieced block; press seam toward strip and trim excess as shown in Figure 4. Continue adding strips in a clockwise direction, pressing and trimming after each addition.

6. Finish pot holder as in General Instructions.

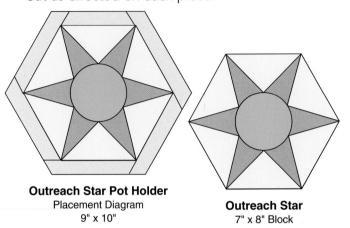

Outreach Star Pot Holder
Placement Diagram
9" x 10"

Outreach Star
7" x 8" Block

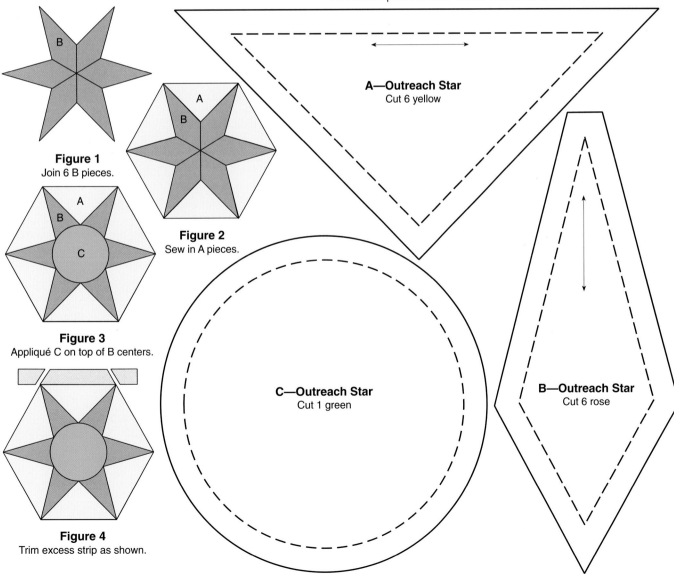

Figure 1
Join 6 B pieces.

Figure 2
Sew in A pieces.

Figure 3
Appliqué C on top of B centers.

Figure 4
Trim excess strip as shown.

A—Outreach Star
Cut 6 yellow

B—Outreach Star
Cut 6 rose

C—Outreach Star
Cut 1 green

Double Star

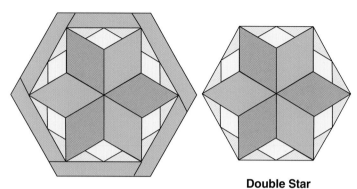

Double Star Pot Holder
Placement Diagram
9" x 10"

Double Star
7" x 8" Block

1. Prepare templates using pattern pieces given. Cut as directed on each piece.

2. To piece block, join green and rose C pieces alternating colors and stitching only to the end of the marked seam allowance.

3. Sew A to two adjacent sides of B as shown in Figure 1; repeat for six units. Set an A-B unit between the points of the C pieces as shown in Figure 2; repeat for all A-B units to complete one block.

4. Sew a border strip to one side of the pieced block; press seam toward strip and trim excess as shown in Figure 3. Continue adding strips in a clockwise direction, pressing and trimming after each addition.

5. Finish pot holder as in General Instructions. ■

Figure 1
Sew A to 2 adjacent sides of B.

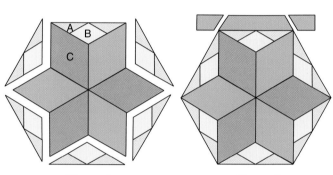

Figure 2
Set an A-B unit
between 2 C points.

Figure 3
Trim excess strip as shown.

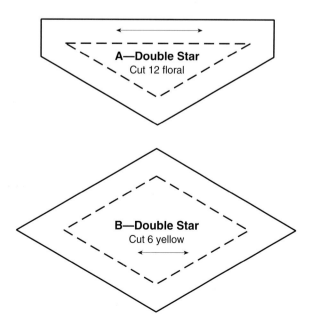

A—Double Star
Cut 12 floral

B—Double Star
Cut 6 yellow

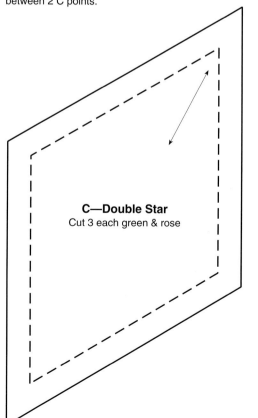

C—Double Star
Cut 3 each green & rose

Beautiful Baskets

Add a collection of baskets to your kitchen.

Block Size

5" x 5"

Fabric

Scraps of the following fabrics: floral print, green, yellow, blue, background

2 strips each 2" x 5½" and 2" x 8½" border fabric

Instructions

Note: Templates on pages 14 and 15.

Basket Quilt

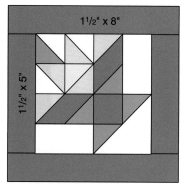

Basket Quilt Pot Holder
Placement Diagram
8" x 8"

Basket Quilt
5" x 5" Block

1. Prepare templates I, J, K, L and M using pattern pieces given on pages 13–15. Cut as directed on each piece for Basket Quilt block.

2. To piece block, sew a yellow L to a background L; repeat. Sew a green L to a background L. Arrange the pieced L units with two yellow and one floral print L triangles as shown in Figure 1; join to make top half of block.

3. Sew a yellow L between M and MR. Sew two green L triangles to adjacent sides of J. Sew to the L-M unit as shown in Figure 2 to make bottom half of block.

4. Sew the remaining green L triangles to K referring to Figure 3.

5. Arrange pieced units with I referring to Figure 3; join to complete one block.

6. Add border strips and finish pot holder as in General Instructions.

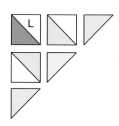

Figure 1
Join L pieces as shown.

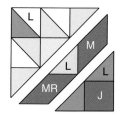

Figure 2
Join units as shown.

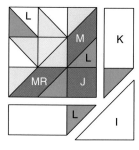

Figure 3
Arrange pieced units as shown.

Dresden Basket

1. Prepare templates I, J, K, L, N, O, P and Q using pattern pieces given on pages 13–15. Cut as directed on each piece for Dresden Basket block.

2. To piece block, sew J to N and yellow L to NR; join these pieced units as shown in Figure 1. Sew Q to P and QR to PR; set onto sides of O. Sew green L to one end of K; repeat, again referring to Figure 1.

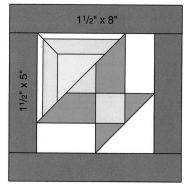

Dresden Basket Pot Holder
Placement Diagram
8" x 8"

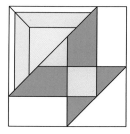

Dresden Basket
5" x 5" Block

3. Arrange the pieced units with I as shown in Figure 2. Join units to complete one block.

4. Add border strips and finish pot holder as in General Instructions.

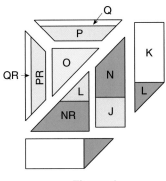

Figure 1
Join pieces as shown.

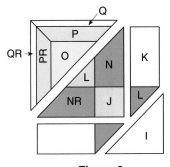

Figure 2
Arrange units as shown.

Flower Pot

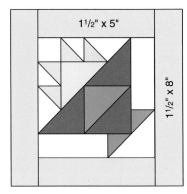

Flower Pot Pot Holder
Placement Diagram
8" x 8"

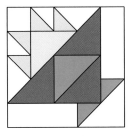

Flower Pot
5" x 5" Block

1. Prepare templates A, B, C, D and E using pattern pieces given on pages 13–15. Cut as directed on each piece for Flower Pot block.

2. To piece block, sew a yellow B triangle to a background B triangle; repeat. Sew a yellow B triangle to one side of E, referring to Figure 1; repeat, again referring to Figure 1.

3. Sew a B-B unit to a B-E unit; repeat. Sew one of these units to one side of the floral print C referring to Figure 2. Sew A to the B-B end of the remaining B-E unit and sew to the previously pieced unit again referring to Figure 2.

4. Join three blue C triangles with one green C triangle as shown in Figure 3. Sew the green B triangles to D, referring to Figure 3.

5. Arrange the pieced units with the background C as shown in Figure 4. Join units to complete one block.

6. Add border strips and finish pot holder as in General Instructions.

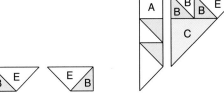

Figure 2
Join units as shown.

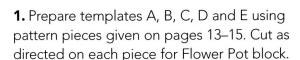

Figure 1
Join pieces as shown.

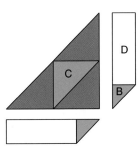

Figure 3
Join pieces as shown.

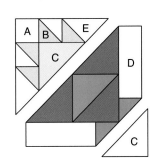

Figure 4
Arrange pieced units as shown.

Spring Basket

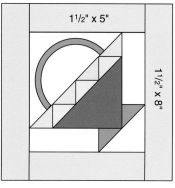

1½" x 5"

1½" x 8"

Spring Basket Pot Holder
Placement Diagram
8" x 8"

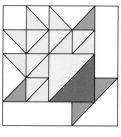

Spring Basket
5" x 5" Block

1. Prepare templates B, C, D, F, G and H using pattern pieces given on pages 13–15. Cut as directed on each piece for Spring Basket block.

2. To piece block, join the floral print B triangles with the yellow B triangles as shown in Figure 1. Sew to the long side of the F triangle.

3. Turn under edges of H; appliqué to G. Sew G-H unit to the B-F unit.

4. Sew a green B triangle to one end of D referring to Figure 2; repeat. Sew to the section pieced in step 3. Sew the C triangle to the corner to finish the block.

5. Add border strips and finish pot holder as in General Instructions.

Figure 1
Join B triangles as shown.

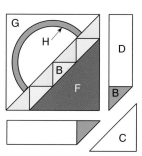

Figure 2
Arrange units as shown.

May Basket

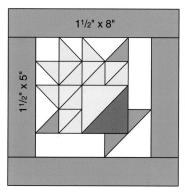

1½" x 8"

1½" x 5"

May Basket Pot Holder
Placement Diagram
8" x 8"

May Basket
5" x 5" Block

1. Prepare templates A, B, C, D and E using pattern pieces given on pages 13–15. Cut as directed on each piece for May Basket block.

2. To piece block, sew a yellow B triangle to a floral print B triangle; repeat for five units. Repeat for two yellow/background B units. Sew yellow and green B triangles to short sides of E; repeat. Sew a floral print C to a blue C. Sew a green B to one end of D; repeat as shown in Figure 1.

3. Arrange the pieced units with remaining background C and A pieces as shown in Figure 2. Join units to complete one block.

4. Add border strips and finish pot holder as in General Instructions.

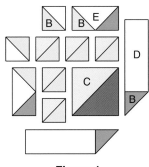

Figure 1
Join pieces as shown.

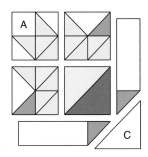

Figure 2
Arrange units as shown.

Cake Stand

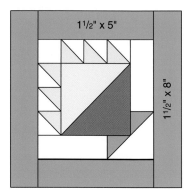

Cake Stand Pot Holder
Placement Diagram
8" x 8"

1½" x 5"

1½" x 8"

Cake Stand
5" x 5" Block

1. Prepare templates A, B, C, D and F using pattern pieces given on pages 13–15. Cut as directed on each piece for Cake Stand block.

2. To piece block, sew a yellow B triangle to background B triangle; repeat for six units. Sew a green B triangle to D; repeat as shown in Figure 1. Join the two F triangles along diagonal side.

3. Arrange the pieced units with remaining background C and A pieces as shown in Figure 2. Join units to complete one block.

4. Add border strips and finish pot holder as in General Instructions. ■

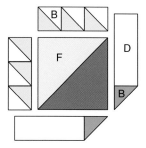

Figure 1
Join pieces as shown.

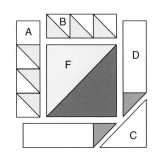

Figure 2
Arrange units as shown.

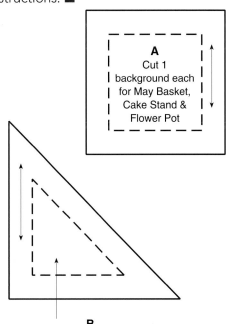

A
Cut 1 background each for May Basket, Cake Stand & Flower Pot

B
Cut 2 background, 4 green, 5 floral print & 9 yellow for May Basket
Cut 2 green & 6 each yellow & background for Cake Stand
Cut 2 each green & background & 4 yellow for Flower Pot
Cut 3 floral print, 2 green & 4 yellow for Spring Basket

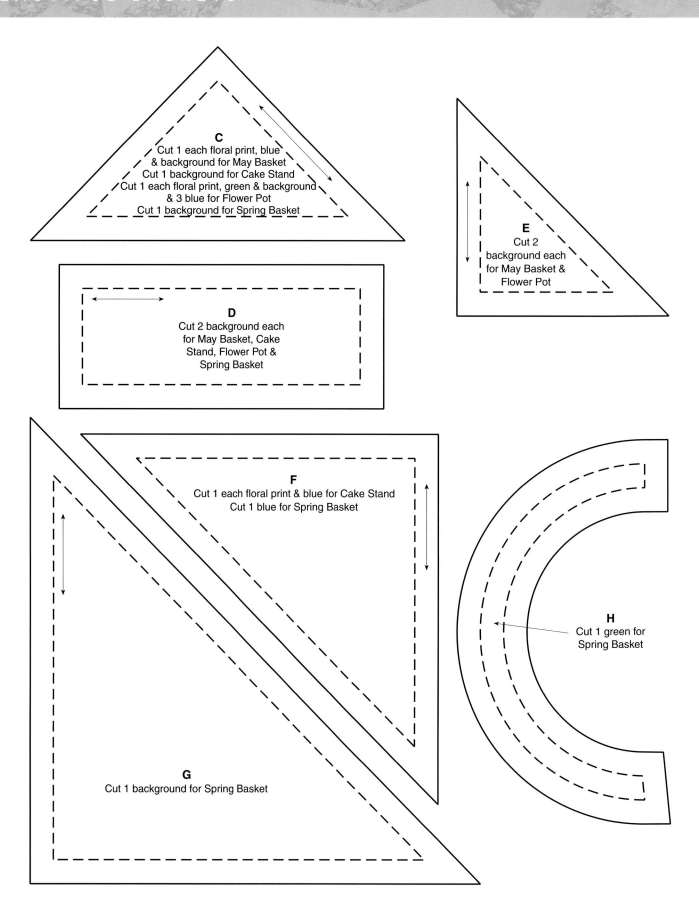

C
Cut 1 each floral print, blue
& background for May Basket
Cut 1 background for Cake Stand
Cut 1 each floral print, green & background
& 3 blue for Flower Pot
Cut 1 background for Spring Basket

E
Cut 2
background each
for May Basket &
Flower Pot

D
Cut 2 background each
for May Basket, Cake
Stand, Flower Pot &
Spring Basket

F
Cut 1 each floral print & blue for Cake Stand
Cut 1 blue for Spring Basket

H
Cut 1 green for
Spring Basket

G
Cut 1 background for Spring Basket

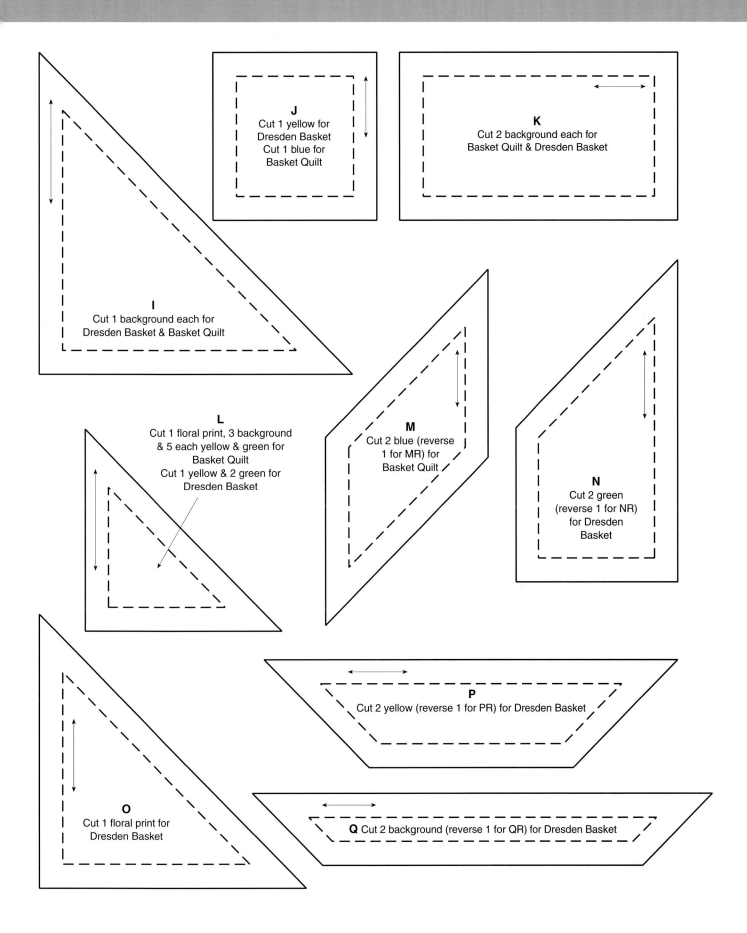

J
Cut 1 yellow for
Dresden Basket
Cut 1 blue for
Basket Quilt

K
Cut 2 background each for
Basket Quilt & Dresden Basket

I
Cut 1 background each for
Dresden Basket & Basket Quilt

L
Cut 1 floral print, 3 background
& 5 each yellow & green for
Basket Quilt
Cut 1 yellow & 2 green for
Dresden Basket

M
Cut 2 blue (reverse
1 for MR) for
Basket Quilt

N
Cut 2 green
(reverse 1 for NR)
for Dresden
Basket

O
Cut 1 floral print for
Dresden Basket

P
Cut 2 yellow (reverse 1 for PR) for Dresden Basket

Q Cut 2 background (reverse 1 for QR) for Dresden Basket

Garden of Flowers

Some flowers blossom only for a day, but these pot holders will bloom forever.

Block Size
8" x 8"

Fabric
Scraps of the following fabrics: background, floral print, light rose, dark rose, blue

Instructions

Garden Favorite

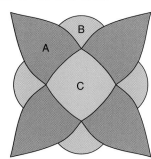

Garden Favorite
Placement Diagram
8" x 8" Block

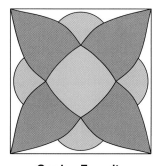

Figure 1
Lay out pieces as shown.

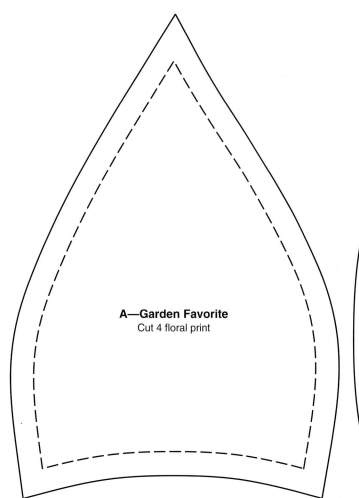

A—Garden Favorite
Cut 4 floral print

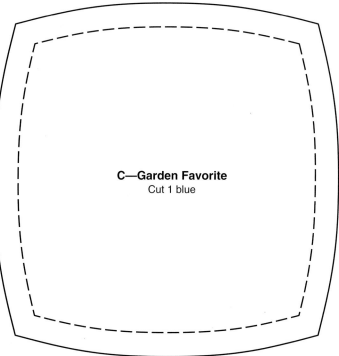

C—Garden Favorite
Cut 1 blue

1. Cut an 8½" x 8½" square background fabric; fold and crease to mark the center.

2. Prepare templates using pattern pieces given. Cut as directed on each piece.

3. Turn under curved edges on A; sew A to each side of C. Turn under curved edges on B; lay out pieces on background block, placing edges of B under edges of A. Appliqué in place.

4. Finish pot holder as in General Instructions.

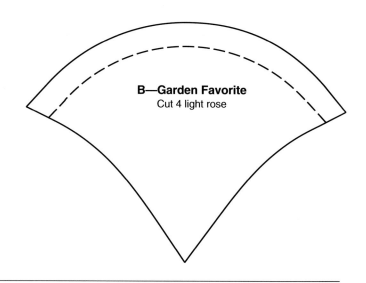

B—Garden Favorite
Cut 4 light rose

Day Lily Garden

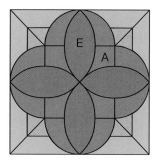

Day Lily Garden
Placement Diagram
8" x 8" Block

1. Prepare templates using pattern pieces given. Cut as directed on each piece.

2. Sew B to C as shown in Figure 1; repeat for four B-C units.

3. Turn under curved edges on D pieces. Sew a D piece to each side of A. Fold D back onto A and sew B-C to the A-D unit along A-D seams. Join B-C units at corners as shown in Figure 2.

4. Fold D back onto B-C; appliqué in place. Turn under edges of E pieces; appliqué on top of A-D area of block with E pieces meeting in the center to complete the block.

5. Finish pot holder as in General Instructions.

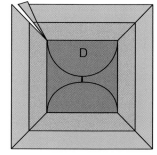

Figure 1
Sew B to C as shown.

Figure 2
Join B-C units at corners.

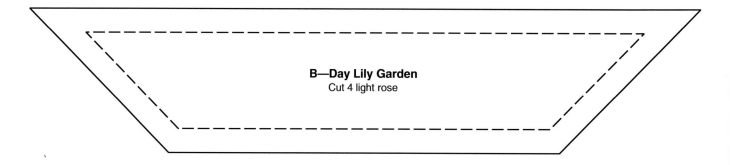

B—Day Lily Garden
Cut 4 light rose

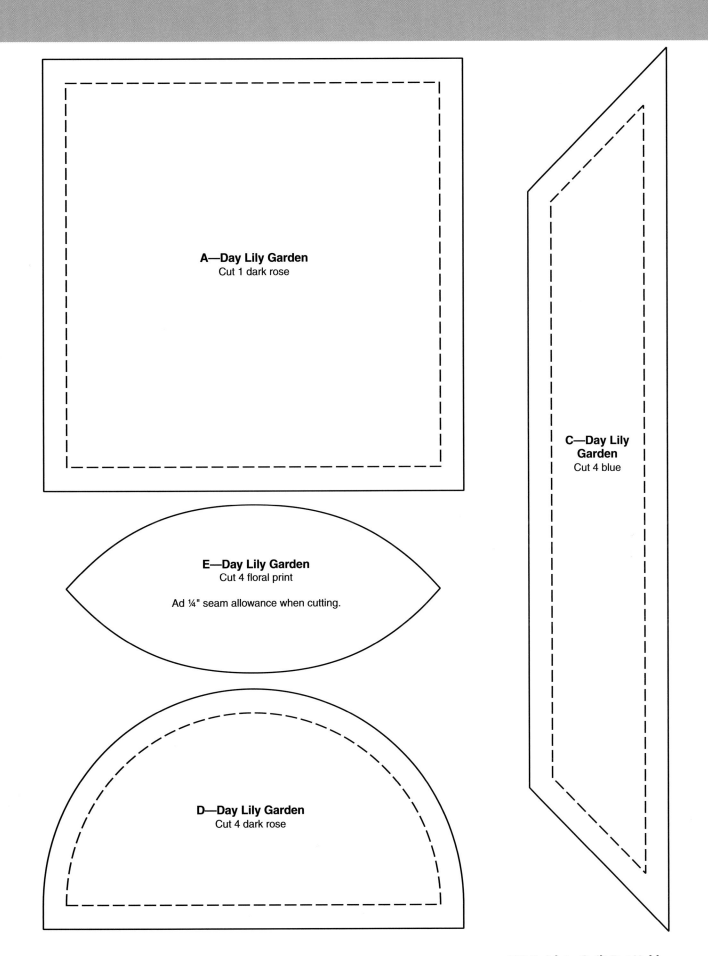

A—Day Lily Garden
Cut 1 dark rose

**C—Day Lily
Garden**
Cut 4 blue

E—Day Lily Garden
Cut 4 floral print

Ad ¼" seam allowance when cutting.

D—Day Lily Garden
Cut 4 dark rose

Morning Flower

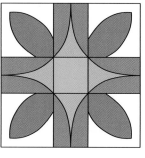

Morning Flower
Placement Diagram
8" x 8" Block

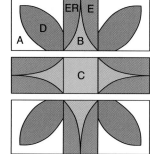

Figure 1
Lay out pieced units in rows as shown.

4. Referring to Figure 1, lay out A-D units with E-B units and C in rows. Join units in rows; join rows to complete block.

5. Finish pot holder as in General Instructions.

1. Prepare templates using pattern pieces given. Cut as directed on each piece.

2. Turn under curved edges on E and ER; appliqué to B. Repeat for four units.

3. Turn under seam allowance on curved edges only of piece D; appliqué to A. Repeat for four units.

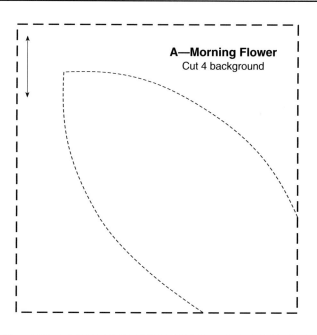

A—Morning Flower
Cut 4 background

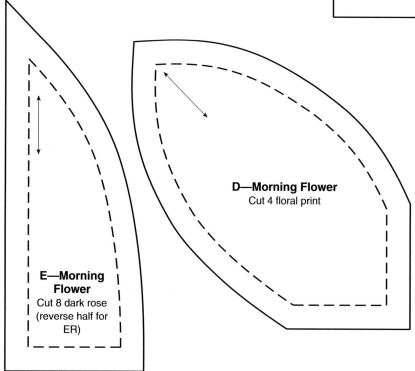

E—Morning Flower
Cut 8 dark rose (reverse half for ER)

D—Morning Flower
Cut 4 floral print

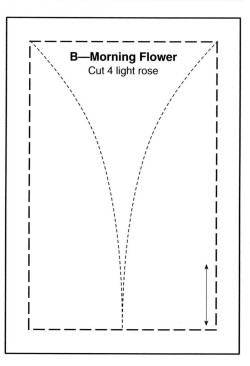

B—Morning Flower
Cut 4 light rose

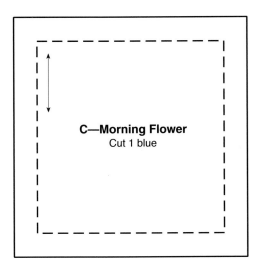

C—Morning Flower
Cut 1 blue

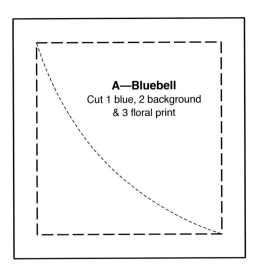

A—Bluebell
Cut 1 blue, 2 background
& 3 floral print

Bluebell

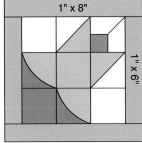

1" x 8"

1" x 6"

Bluebell Pot Holder
Placement Diagram
8" x 8"

Bluebell
6" x 6" Block

E—Bluebell
Cut 2 blue

B—Bluebell
Cut 2 each blue & background

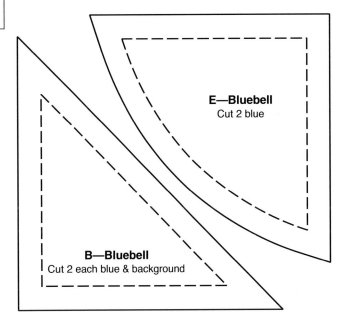

1. Prepare templates using pattern pieces given. Cut as directed on each piece.

2. Turn under curved edge on E; appliqué to A; repeat. Sew a background B to a blue B; repeat. Sew C and CR to D.

C—Bluebell
Cut 2 background
(reverse 1 for CR)

3. Arrange pieced units in rows referring to Figure 1. Join in rows; join rows to complete block.

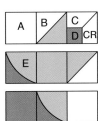

A B C
        D CR

E

D—Bluebell
Cut 1 dark rose

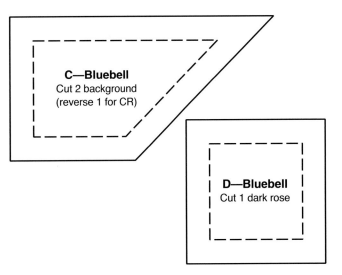

4. Finish pot holder as in General Instructions.

Figure 1
Lay out pieced units
in rows as shown.

Dogtooth Violet

1. Prepare templates using pattern pieces given. Cut as directed on each piece.

2. Sew two D pieces to C; repeat for four C-D units. Sew C-D units to E. Sew A and AR to B, sewing only to the end of the marked seam line. Set in A-B-AR units at sides to complete the block as shown in Figure 1.

3. Finish pot holder as in General Instructions.

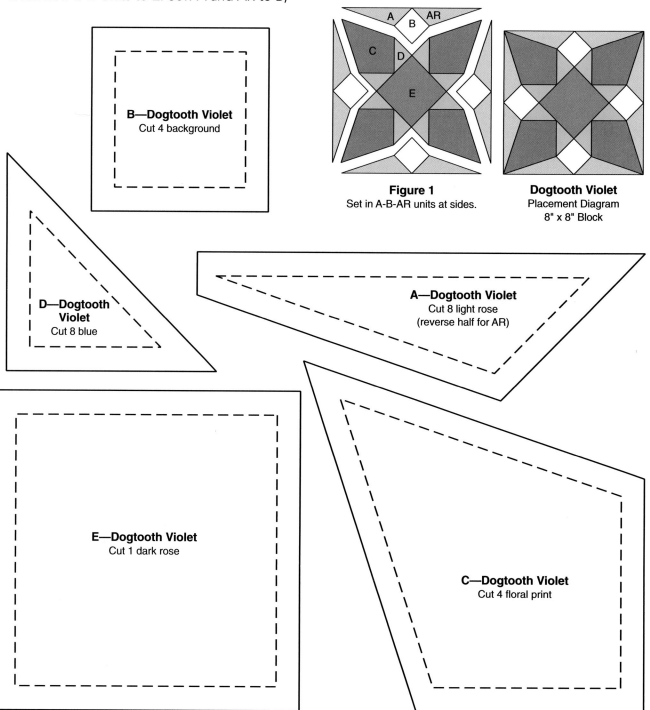

Figure 1
Set in A-B-AR units at sides.

Dogtooth Violet
Placement Diagram
8" x 8" Block

B—Dogtooth Violet
Cut 4 background

D—Dogtooth Violet
Cut 8 blue

A—Dogtooth Violet
Cut 8 light rose
(reverse half for AR)

E—Dogtooth Violet
Cut 1 dark rose

C—Dogtooth Violet
Cut 4 floral print

Honey Bee

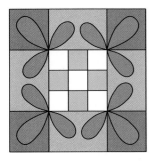

Honey Bee
Placement Diagram
7" x 7" Block

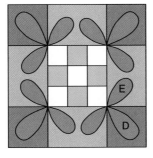

Honey Bee
7" x 7" Block

3. Sew A to B to A; repeat. Sew remaining two B pieces to opposite sides of the pieced Nine-Patch. Sew the A-B-A units to the remaining sides referring to Figure 2.

4. Turn under edges of D and E pieces. Appliqué D on A squares and E on B rectangles referring to the block drawing.

5. Finish pot holder as in General Instructions. ■

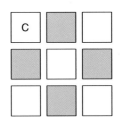

Figure 1
Join C pieces to make
Nine-Patch center.

1. Prepare templates using pattern pieces given. Cut as directed on each piece.

2. Sew C pieces together to make a Nine-Patch center referring to Figure 1.

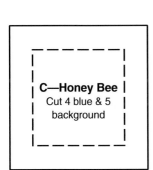

C—Honey Bee
Cut 4 blue & 5
background

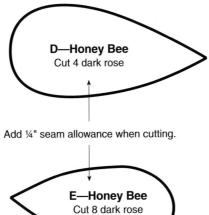

D—Honey Bee
Cut 4 dark rose

Add ¼" seam allowance when cutting.

E—Honey Bee
Cut 8 dark rose

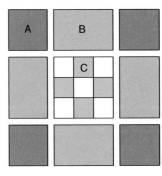

Figure 2
Arrange pieced units as shown.

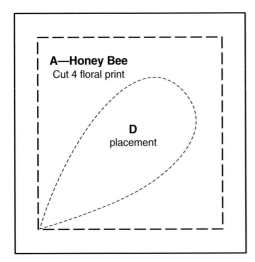

A—Honey Bee
Cut 4 floral print

D
placement

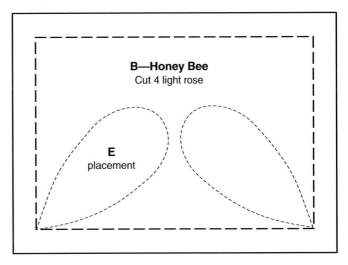

B—Honey Bee
Cut 4 light rose

E
placement

Patriotic Mosaics

Add a touch of patriotism to your dining with this collection of red, white and blue pot holders.

Block Size
6" x 6"

Fabric
Scraps of the following fabrics: white, floral, navy, red
2 strips each 1½" x 6½" and 1½" x 8½" border fabric

Instructions
Note: Templates on pages 35 and 36.

2. To piece block, sew three floral and one navy D triangles together as shown in Figure 1; repeat for four units.

3. Sew I to each side of J as shown in Figure 2.

4. Sew a pieced D unit to each side of the I-J unit to complete one block as shown in Figure 3.

5. Add border strips and finish pot holder as in General Instructions.

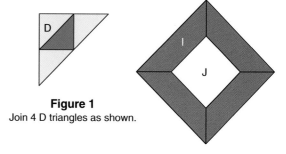

Figure 1
Join 4 D triangles as shown.

Figure 2
Sew I to each side of J.

Mosaic

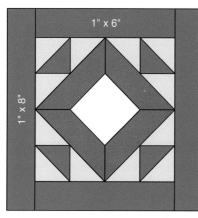

Mosaic 21 Pot Holder
Placement Diagram
8" x 8"

Mosaic 21
6" x 6" Block

1. Prepare templates for pieces D, I and J using pattern pieces given on pages 35 and 36. Cut as directed on each piece for the Mosaic block.

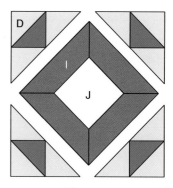

Figure 3
Sew the pieced D units to the I-J unit to complete 1 block.

Spinning Star

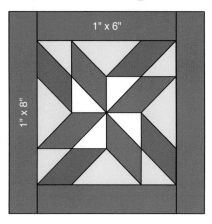

Spinning Star Pot Holder
Placement Diagram
8" x 8"

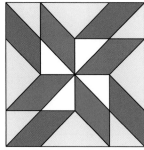

Spinning Star
6" x 6" Block

each color combination. Sew a red/floral unit to a navy/white unit as shown in Figure 1; repeat for four units.

3. Join the four pieced units and set in A triangles as shown in Figure 2 to complete one block.

4. Add border strips and finish pot holder as in General Instructions.

1. Prepare templates for pieces A, D and K using pattern pieces given on pages 35 and 36. Cut as directed on each piece for the Spinning Star block.

2. To piece block, sew a white D to a navy K and a floral D to a red K; repeat for four of

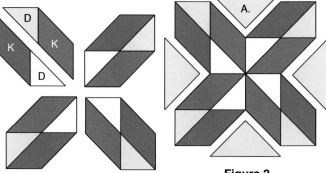

Figure 1
Sew pieced units together as shown.

Figure 2
Join 4 pieced units; set in A to complete 1 block.

Mosaic Pinwheel

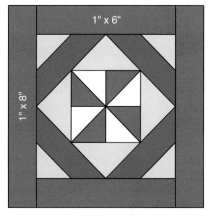

Mosaic Pinwheel Pot Holder
Placement Diagram
8" x 8"

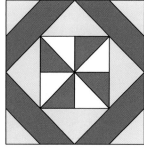

Mosaic Pinwheel
6" x 6" Block

1. Prepare templates for pieces A, D and I using pattern pieces given on pages 35 and 36. Cut as directed on each piece for the Mosaic Pinwheel block.

2. To piece block, sew a white D to a red D; repeat for four units. Join these units as shown in Figure 1 to make pinwheel center.

3. Sew an A triangle to each side of the pinwheel unit.

4. Sew D to I; repeat for four units. Sew a D-I unit to each side of the A-D unit as shown in Figure 2 to complete one block.

5. Add border strips and finish pot holder as in General Instructions.

Figure 1
Join the D units to
make a pinwheel unit.

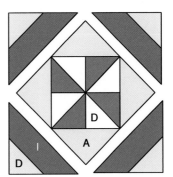

Figure 2
Sew a D-I unit to each side of
the A-D unit to complete 1 block.

Windblown Square

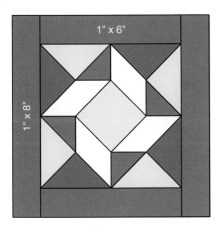

Windblown Square Pot Holder
Placement Diagram
8" x 8"

1. Prepare templates for pieces A, D, J and K using pattern pieces given on pages 35 and 36. Cut as directed on each piece for the Windblown Square block.

2. To piece block, sew D to K as shown in Figure 1; repeat for four units. Sew one of these units to each side of J as shown in Figure 2.

3. Sew a navy A to a floral A as shown in Figure 3; repeat for four units. Sew one of these units to each side of the D-J-K unit to complete one block again referring to Figure 3.

4. Add border strips and finish pot holder as in General Instructions.

Figure 1
Sew D to K.

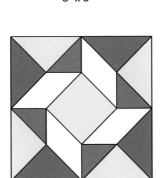

Windblown Square
6" x 6" Block

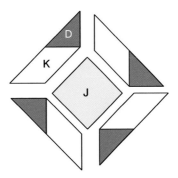

Figure 2
Sew the D-K units to each side of J.

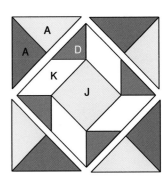

Figure 3
Sew the A-A units to each side of the
D-J-K unit to complete 1 block.

Wheels

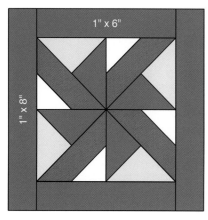

Wheels Potholder
Placement Diagram
8" x 8"

Wheels
6" x 6" Block

Figure 1
Sew A to A as shown.

Figure 2
Sew an I-D unit to an A-A unit.

1. Prepare templates for pieces A, D and I using pattern pieces given on pages 35 and 36. Cut as directed on each piece for the Wheels block.

2. To piece block, sew A to A as shown in Figure 1; repeat for four units. Sew I to D; repeat for four units.

3. Sew an I-D unit to an A-A unit as shown in Figure 2; repeat for four units.

4. Join the four pieced units as shown in Figure 3 to complete one block.

5. Add border strips and finish pot holder as in General Instructions.

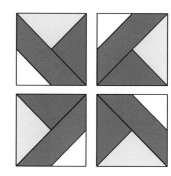

Figure 3
Join the 4 pieced units to complete 1 block.

Bachelor's Puzzle

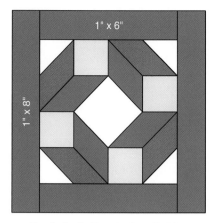

1" x 6"

1" x 8"

Bachelor's Puzzle Pot Holder
Placement Diagram
8" x 8"

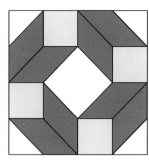

Bachelor's Puzzle
6" x 6" Block

1. Prepare templates for pieces C, D, J and K using pattern pieces given on pages 35 and 36. Cut as directed on each piece for the Bachelor's Puzzle block.

2. To piece block, sew navy K to red KR, sewing to the end of the marked seam line; repeat for four units.

3. Sew C into a K-KR unit as shown in Figure 1; repeat for four units. Sew a D triangle to KR side of each unit as shown in Figure 2.

4. Sew a pieced unit to each side of J in a clockwise direction as shown in Figure 3.

5. Add border strips and finish pot holder as in General Instructions. ■

Figure 1
Sew C into a K-KR unit.

Figure 2
Sew D to the pieced
unit as shown.

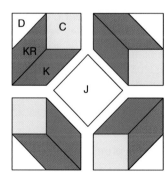

Figure 3
Sew a pieced unit to each side
of J to complete 1 block.

Chocolate Confections

Set the mood for dining with these chocolate-inspired confections.

Block Size
6" x 6"

Fabric
Scraps of the following fabrics: white, floral, blue, brown
2 strips each 1½" x 6½" and 1½" x 8½" border fabric

Instructions
Note: *Templates on pages 35 and 36.*

Mosaic Square

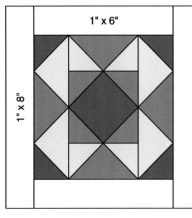

Mosaic Square
Placement Diagram
8" x 8"

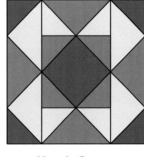

Mosaic Square
6" x 6" Block

1. Prepare templates for pieces A, D and J using pattern pieces given on pages 35 and 36. Cut as directed on each piece for the Mosaic Square block.

2. To piece block, sew four blue D triangles to J. Sew two floral D triangles to a blue A; repeat. Sew with the D sides to the D-J unit as shown in Figure 1.

3. Sew two floral A triangles to a blue A triangle; sew a brown D triangle to each end as shown in Figure 2. Repeat for two units. Sew one of these units to each of the opposite long sides of the previously pieced unit as shown in Figure 3 to complete one block.

4. Add border strips and finish pot holder as in General Instructions.

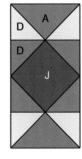

Figure 1
Sew the A-D units to the
D-J unit as shown.

Figure 2
Sew a D triangle to each
end of an A unit.

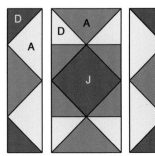

Figure 3
Sew the A-D units to opposite
sides of the pieced center.

Missouri Star

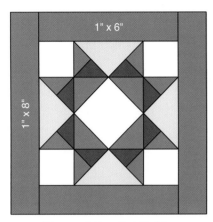

Missouri Star Pot Holder
Placement Diagram
8" x 8"

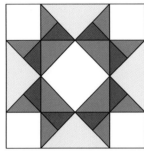

Missouri Star
6" x 6" Block

1. Prepare templates for pieces A, C, D, J and O using pattern pieces given on pages 35 and 36. Cut as directed on each piece for the Missouri Star block.

2. To piece block, sew four blue D triangles to J. Sew a blue O to a brown O as shown in Figure 1; repeat for eight units. Sew two O units to A as shown in Figure 2; repeat for four units.

3. Sew an A-O unit to opposite sides of the D-J unit as shown in Figure 3. Sew C to each end of the remaining A-O units. Sew these units to the previously pieced unit to complete one block as shown in Figure 4.

4. Add border strips and finish pot holder as in General Instructions.

Figure 1
Sew 2 O triangles together.

Figure 2
Sew 2 O units to A.

Figure 3
Sew an A-O unit to opposite sides of the D-J unit.

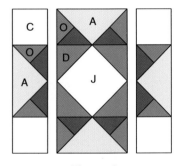

Figure 4
Sew A-C-O units to pieced unit to complete 1 block.

Mosaic Star

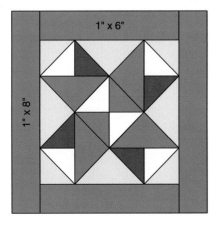

Mosaic Star Pot Holder
Placement Diagram
8" x 8"

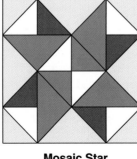

Mosaic Star
6" x 6" Block

1. Prepare templates for pieces A and D using pattern pieces given on pages 35 and 36. Cut as directed on each piece for the Mosaic Star block.

2. To piece block, join two white and two blue D triangles as shown in Figure 1 for center.

3. Sew a white D to a brown D to a blue A as shown in Figure 2; sew a floral D to the white D side as shown in Figure 3; repeat for four units. Sew one of these units to each of the blue sides of the pieced center as shown in Figure 4.

4. Sew a floral A to opposite sides of the remaining A-D units as shown in Figure 5. Sew these units to the long sides of the previously pieced unit to complete one block.

5. Add border strips and finish pot holder as in General Instructions.

Figure 1
Sew D pieces together as shown for center.

Figure 2
Sew 2 D triangles to A.

Figure 3
Sew a floral D to the white D side of the A-D unit.

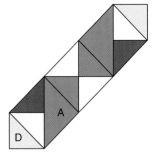

Figure 4
Sew an A-D unit to the blue sides of the center unit.

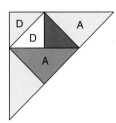

Figure 5
Sew A to the pieced A-D unit. Sew to previously pieced unit as shown.

Home Treasure

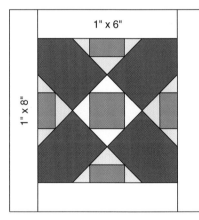

Home Treasure Pot Holders
Placement Diagram
8" x 8"

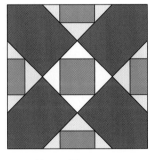

Home Treasure
6" x 6" Block

1. Prepare templates for pieces C, O, P, Q and R using pattern pieces given on pages 35 and 36. Cut as directed on each piece for the Home Treasure block.

2. To piece block, sew four white O triangles to C; sew an R to two opposite sides of the C-O unit as shown in Figure 1.

3. Sew Q to P to Q to floral O as shown in Figure 2; repeat for four units. Sew two of these units to R as shown in Figure 3; repeat.

4. Sew the O-P-Q-R units to opposite sides of the previously pieced C-O-R unit to complete one block as shown in Figure 4.

5. Add border strips and finish pot holder as in General Instructions.

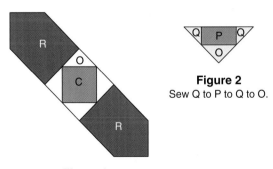

Figure 1
Sew R to 2 opposite sides of the C-O unit.

Figure 2
Sew Q to P to Q to O.

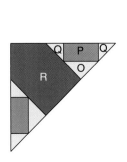

Figure 3
Sew 2 O-P-Q units to R.

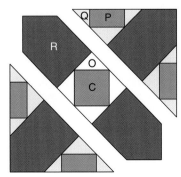

Figure 4
Join pieced units.

Four Squares

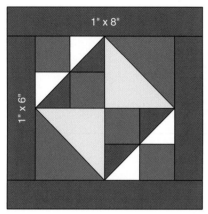

1" x 8"

1" x 6"

Four Squares Pot Holder
Placement Diagram
8" x 8"

Four Squares
6" x 6" Block

1. Prepare templates for pieces B, C and D using pattern pieces given on pages 35 and 36. Cut as directed on each piece for the Four Squares block.

2. To piece block, sew a white D to a brown D; repeat for four units. Sew C to two white D sides and to two brown D sides. Join two of these units as shown in Figure 1; repeat.

3. Sew a floral B to a blue B along diagonal sides; repeat.

4. Arrange units as shown in Figure 2; join to complete one block.

5. Add border strips and finish pot holder as in General Instructions.

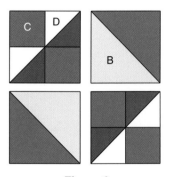

Figure 1
Join pieced units as shown.

Figure 2
Arrange pieced units
to make 1 block.

Coxey's Camp

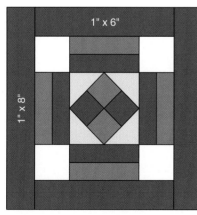

1" x 6"

1" x 8"

Coxey's Camp Pot Holder
Placement Diagram
8" x 8"

Coxey's Camp
6" x 6" Block

1. Prepare templates for pieces C, D, M and N using pattern pieces given on pages 35 and 36. Cut as directed on each piece for the Coxey's Camp block.

2. To piece block, sew a blue N to a brown N; repeat. Join these two units to make a Four-Patch. Sew a floral D triangle to each side.

3. Sew a brown M to a blue M; repeat for four units. Sew one of these units to two opposite sides of the D-N unit.

4. Sew a white C square to each end of the remaining M units. Sew one of these units to opposite long sides of the previously pieced unit to complete one block as shown in Figure 1.

5. Add border strips and finish pot holder as in General Instructions. ■

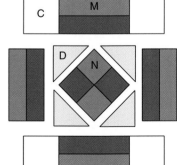

Figure 1
Join units as shown.

Templates (for pages 24–34)

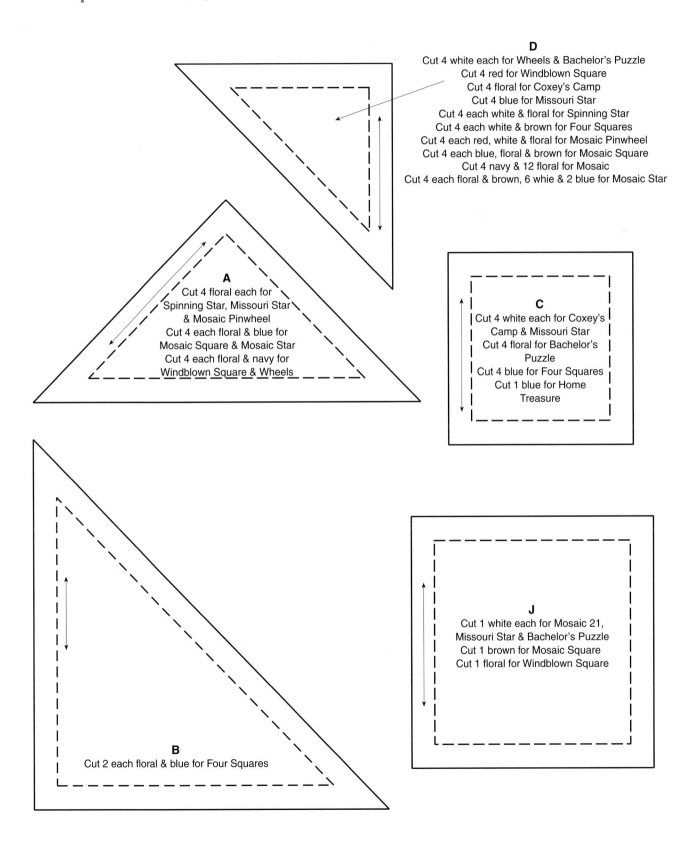

D
Cut 4 white each for Wheels & Bachelor's Puzzle
Cut 4 red for Windblown Square
Cut 4 floral for Coxey's Camp
Cut 4 blue for Missouri Star
Cut 4 each white & floral for Spinning Star
Cut 4 each white & brown for Four Squares
Cut 4 each red, white & floral for Mosaic Pinwheel
Cut 4 each blue, floral & brown for Mosaic Square
Cut 4 navy & 12 floral for Mosaic
Cut 4 each floral & brown, 6 whie & 2 blue for Mosaic Star

A
Cut 4 floral each for
Spinning Star, Missouri Star
& Mosaic Pinwheel
Cut 4 each floral & blue for
Mosaic Square & Mosaic Star
Cut 4 each floral & navy for
Windblown Square & Wheels

C
Cut 4 white each for Coxey's
Camp & Missouri Star
Cut 4 floral for Bachelor's
Puzzle
Cut 4 blue for Four Squares
Cut 1 blue for Home
Treasure

B
Cut 2 each floral & blue for Four Squares

J
Cut 1 white each for Mosaic 21,
Missouri Star & Bachelor's Puzzle
Cut 1 brown for Mosaic Square
Cut 1 floral for Windblown Square

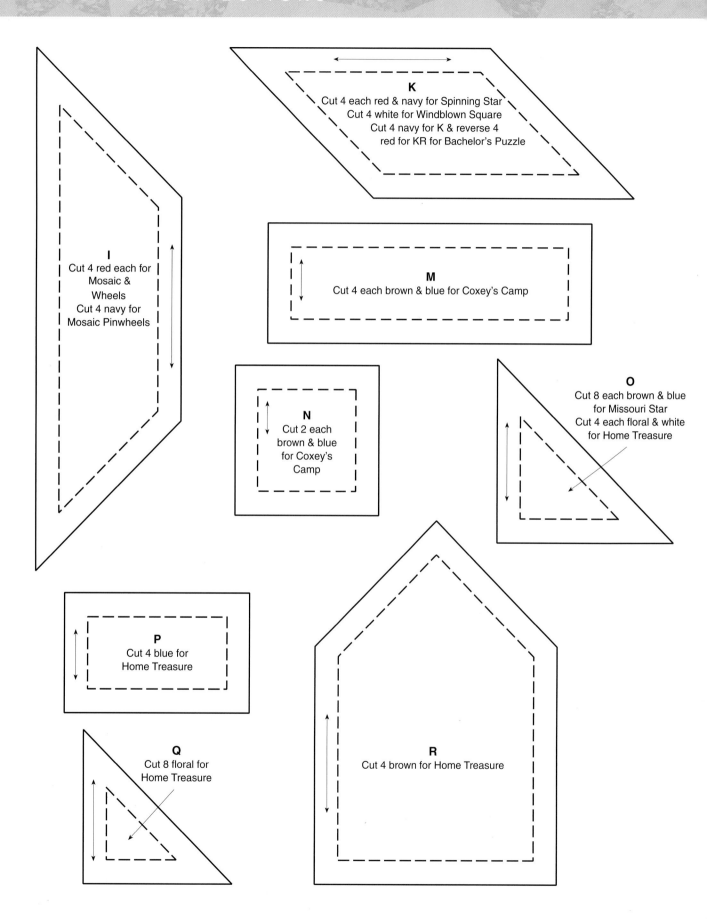

K
Cut 4 each red & navy for Spinning Star
Cut 4 white for Windblown Square
Cut 4 navy for K & reverse 4
red for KR for Bachelor's Puzzle

I
Cut 4 red each for
Mosaic &
Wheels
Cut 4 navy for
Mosaic Pinwheels

M
Cut 4 each brown & blue for Coxey's Camp

N
Cut 2 each
brown & blue
for Coxey's
Camp

O
Cut 8 each brown & blue
for Missouri Star
Cut 4 each floral & white
for Home Treasure

P
Cut 4 blue for
Home Treasure

Q
Cut 8 floral for
Home Treasure

R
Cut 4 brown for Home Treasure

Culinary Delights

Brighten your kitchen with these delightful pieced pot holders.

Block Sizes

6" x 6" and 12" x 12"

Fabric

Scraps of the following fabrics: red, red print, green, green print, green leaf, yellow floral, small floral, blue, blue print, blue floral, light blue print, dark blue print, pink, rose, rust

Instructions

Note: *Use templates on pages 46–49. Prepare templates needed for your selected pot holder. Cut pieces for individual pot holder following the color diagram and/or the piecing instructions.*

Fizzle

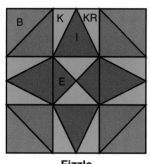
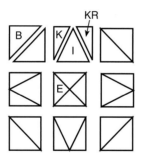

Fizzle
6" x 6" Block

Templates needed:
B, E, I, K & KR

1. Referring to the Piecing Diagram, sew a green leaf B to a red B along the diagonal to make a corner unit; repeat for four corner units.

2. Sew a green print K and KR to a red print I to make a side unit; repeat for four side units.

3. Join two red print and two green print E triangles to make the center unit.

4. Arrange the units in rows referring to the Piecing Diagram. Join units in rows; join rows to complete one block.

5. Finish pot holder as in General Instructions.

Handy Andy

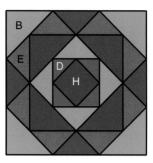

Handy Andy
6" x 6" Block

Templates needed:
B, D, E & H

1. Referring to the Piecing Diagram, sew a green leaf D to each side of a yellow floral H square; sew a green E to each side of this pieced unit and a yellow floral B to each side of the resulting unit to complete the block center.

2. Join two small floral E triangles with one rust E to make a side unit; repeat for four side units.

3. Sew a side unit to each side of the pieced center. Sew a green B triangle to each side of the pieced unit to complete one block.

4. Finish pot holder as in General Instructions.

Snowball Variation

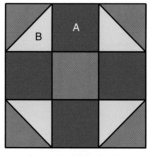
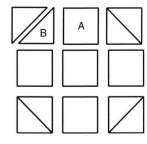

Snowball Variation
6" x 6" Block

Templates needed:
A & B

1. Referring to the Piecing Diagram, sew a blue B to a blue print B along the diagonal to make a corner unit; repeat for four corner units.

2. Arrange the corner units in rows with one blue print and four green floral A pieces referring to the Piecing Diagram.

3. Join units and pieces in rows; join rows to complete one block.

4. Finish pot holder as in General Instructions.

Paths & Stiles

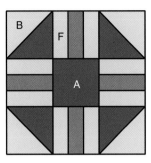

Paths & Stiles
6" x 6" Block

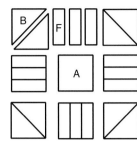

Templates needed:
A, B & F

1. Referring to the Piecing Diagram, sew a light blue print B to a dark blue print B along the diagonal to complete one corner unit; repeat for four corner units.

2. Sew a blue print F between two light blue print F pieces to complete one side unit; repeat for four side units.

3. Arrange the side and corner units in rows with a dark blue print A square referring to the Piecing Diagram. Join units in rows; join rows to complete one block.

4. Finish pot holder as in General Instructions.

Rolling Stone

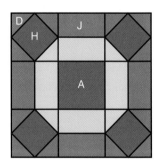

Rolling Stone
12" x 12" Block

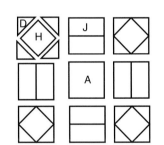

Templates needed:
A, D, H & J

1. Referring to the Piecing Diagram, sew one blue print and three blue D pieces to the sides of a blue floral H to complete one corner unit; repeat for four corner units.

2. Sew a blue J to a blue print J to complete one side unit; repeat for four side units.

3. Arrange the side and corner units in rows with a blue floral A referring to the Piecing Diagram. Join units in rows; join rows to complete one block.

4. Finish pot holder as in General Instructions.

Contrary Wife

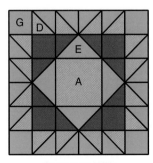

Contrary Wife
6" x 6" Block

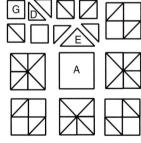

Templates needed:
A, D, E & G

1. Referring to the Piecing Diagram, sew a pink D to a green print D along the diagonal; repeat for 16 units.

2. Join two D units with one each rose and green print G squares to make a corner unit; repeat for four corner units.

3. Sew a rose D to two adjacent sides of a green print E. Join two D units and sew to the D-E unit to complete a side unit; repeat for four side units.

4. Arrange the pieced units in rows with a pink A square referring to the Piecing Diagram. Join units in rows; join rows to complete one block.

5. Finish pot holder as in General Instructions.

Grandma's Star

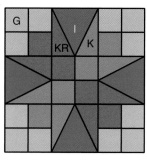

Grandma's Star
6" x 6" Block

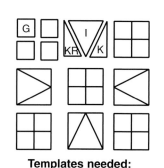

Templates needed:
G, I, K & KR

1. Referring to the Piecing Diagram, join one rust and three small floral G squares to make a Four-Patch corner unit; repeat for four corner units. Join two rust and two red G squares to make one Four-Patch center unit.

2. Sew a red K and a rust KR to the sides of a yellow floral I to make a side unit; repeat for four side units.

3. Arrange the units in rows referring to the Piecing Diagram. Join units in rows; join rows to complete one block.

4. Finish pot holder as in General Instructions.

Treasure Chest

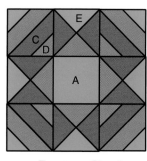

Treasure Chest
6" x 6" Block

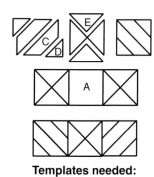

Templates needed:
A, C, D & E

1. Referring to the Piecing Diagram, sew a rust D to a red C; repeat for four units.

2. Sew a green D to a rust C; repeat for four units.

3. Join one of each color version of the C-D units to complete one corner unit; repeat for four corner units.

4. Join one green, one rust and two red E triangles to make a side unit; repeat for four side units.

5. Arrange the pieced units in rows with one green A square referring to the Piecing Diagram. Join units in rows; join rows to complete one block.

6. Finish pot holder as in General Instructions.

Blossom

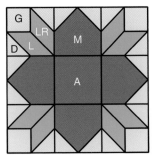

Blossom
12" x 12" Block

Templates needed:
A, D, G, L, LR & M

1. Referring to the Piecing Diagram, sew a green floral L to a green floral LR; sew a blue print D to L and LR. Set in a blue print G to complete one corner unit. Repeat for four corner units..

2. Sew a blue print D to the angled sides of a blue floral M to complete a side unit; repeat for four side units.

3. Arrange the pieced units in rows with a blue floral A square referring to the Piecing Diagram. Join units in rows; join rows to complete one block.

4. Finish pot holder as in General Instructions.

1. Referring to the Piecing Diagram, sew a blue print B to a dark blue print B along the diagonal to make a corner unit; repeat for four corner units.

2. Join two blue print and two dark blue print E triangles to make a side unit; repeat for four side units.

3. Arrange the units in rows with a blue print A square referring to the Piecing Diagram. Join units in rows; join rows to complete one block.

4. Finish pot holder as in General Instructions.

London Roads

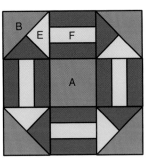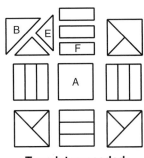

London Roads
12" x 12" Block

Templates needed:
A, B, E & F

1. Referring to the Piecing Diagram, join a light blue print E with a dark blue print E along the short sides; add a blue print B to make a corner unit. Repeat for four corner units.

2. Sew a light blue print F between two dark blue print F pieces to make a side unit; repeat for four side units.

3. Arrange the pieced units in rows with a blue print A square referring to the Piecing Diagram. Join units in rows; join rows to complete one block.

4. Finish pot holder as in General Instructions. ◼

Four-X

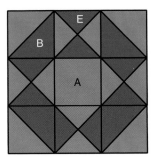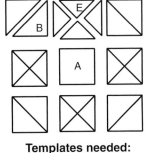

Four-X
6" x 6" Block

Templates needed:
A, B & E

Melon Patch

Hospitality begins with a slice of something sweet.

Block Sizes
6" x 6" and 12" x 12"

Fabric
Scraps of the following fabrics: red print, blue print, blue check, green print, green plaid, leaf print, watermelon print, green stripe, white, orange print, melon print

Instructions
Note: *Use templates on pages 46–49. Prepare templates needed for your selected pot holder. Cut pieces for individual pot holder following the color diagram and/or the piecing instructions.*

Churn Dash

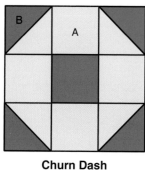

Churn Dash
6" x 6" Block

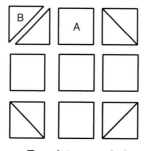

Templates needed:
A & B

1. Referring to the Piecing Diagram, sew a red print B to a leaf print B along the diagonal to complete a corner unit; repeat for four corner units.

2. Arrange the pieced units in rows with one red print and four leaf print A squares referring to the Piecing Diagram. Join units in rows; join rows to complete one block.

3. Finish pot holder as in General Instructions.

Jackknife Variation

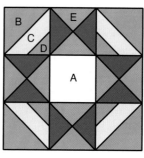

Jackknife Variation
12" x 12" Block

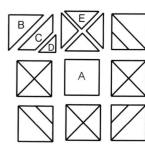

Templates needed:
A, B, C, D & E

1. Referring to the Piecing Diagram, sew a blue plaid B to a melon print C to a blue plaid D to complete one corner unit; repeat for four corner units.

2. Join two blue plaid and two blue print E triangles to complete one side unit; repeat for four side units.

3. Arrange the pieced units in rows with a watermelon print A square referring to the Piecing Diagram. Join units in rows; join rows to complete one block.

4. Finish pot holder as in General Instructions.

Country Farm

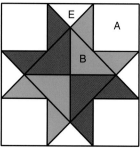

Country Farm
12" x 12" Block

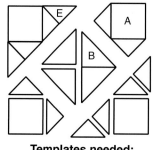

Templates needed:
A, B & E

1. Referring to the Piecing Diagram, join two blue print and two green print B triangles to complete the block center.

2. Sew two blue print E triangles to two adjacent sides of a watermelon print A; repeat for two units. Sew a unit to opposite sides of the block center.

3. Sew two green print E triangles to two adjacent sides of a watermelon print A; repeat for two units. Sew a watermelon print E to each end of each A-E unit to complete large corner units.

4. Sew a large corner unit to each long side of the previously pieced unit to complete one block.

5. Finish pot holder as in General Instructions.

Ohio Star

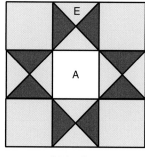

Ohio Star
6" x 6" Block

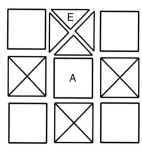

Templates needed:
A & E

1. Referring to the Piecing Diagram, join one leaf print, one green stripe and two red print E triangles to make a side unit; repeat for four side units.

2. Arrange pieced units in rows with one watermelon print and four leaf print A squares referring to the Piecing Diagram. Join units in rows; join rows to complete one block.

3. Finish pot holder as in General Instructions.

Card Trick

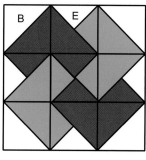

Card Trick
12" x 12" Block

Templates needed:
B & E

1. Referring to the Piecing Diagram, sew a watermelon B to a blue print B along the diagonal to complete one corner unit; repeat for two corner units. Repeat with a watermelon B and a green print B to complete two more corner units.

2. Sew a green print E to a watermelon E on the short sides; add a blue print B to the long side of the pieced unit to complete a side unit. Repeat for two side units. Repeat with blue print and watermelon E triangles and a green print B to complete two more side units.

3. Join two green print and two blue print E triangles to complete the center unit.

4. Arrange the pieced units in rows referring to the Piecing Diagram. Join units in rows; join rows to complete one block.

5. Finish pot holder as in General Instructions.

Antique Tile

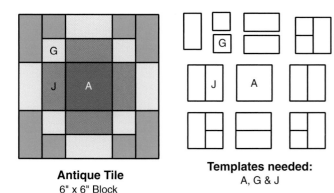

Antique Tile
6" x 6" Block

Templates needed:
A, G & J

1. Referring to the Piecing Diagram, join a green plaid and melon print J; repeat for four units.

2. Join a green print and green plaid G; repeat for four units. Sew a green print J piece to each G-G unit for four corner units.

3. Arrange the pieced units in rows with a green print A referring to the Piecing Diagram. Join units in rows; join rows to complete one block.

4. Finish pot holder as in General Instructions.

Judy in Arabia

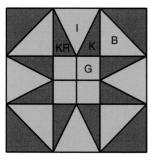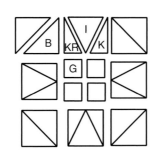

Judy in Arabia
6" x 6" Block

Templates needed:
B, G, I, K & KR

1. Referring to the Piecing Diagram, sew a red print B to an orange print B along the diagonal to make a corner unit; repeat for four corner units.

2. Sew a red print K and KR to the angled sides of an orange print I to make a side unit; repeat for four side units.

3. Sew four orange print G squares together to make the Four-Patch center unit.

4. Arrange the units in rows referring to the Piecing Diagram. Join units in rows; join rows to complete one block.

5. Finish pot holder as in General Instructions.

Crow's Nest

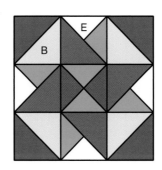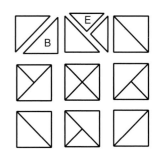

Crow's Nest
12" x 12" Block

Templates needed:
B & E

1. Referring to the Piecing Diagram, sew a green plaid B to a leaf print B along the diagonal; repeat for four units.

2. Sew a white E to a green plaid E on the short sides; sew a green print B to the long side of the E-E unit to complete a side unit. Repeat for four side units.

3. Join two green plaid and two print E triangles to complete the center unit.

4. Arrange the pieced units in rows referring to the Piecing Diagram. Join units in rows; join rows to complete one block.

5. Finish pot holder as in General Instructions. ■

Templates (for pages 37–45)

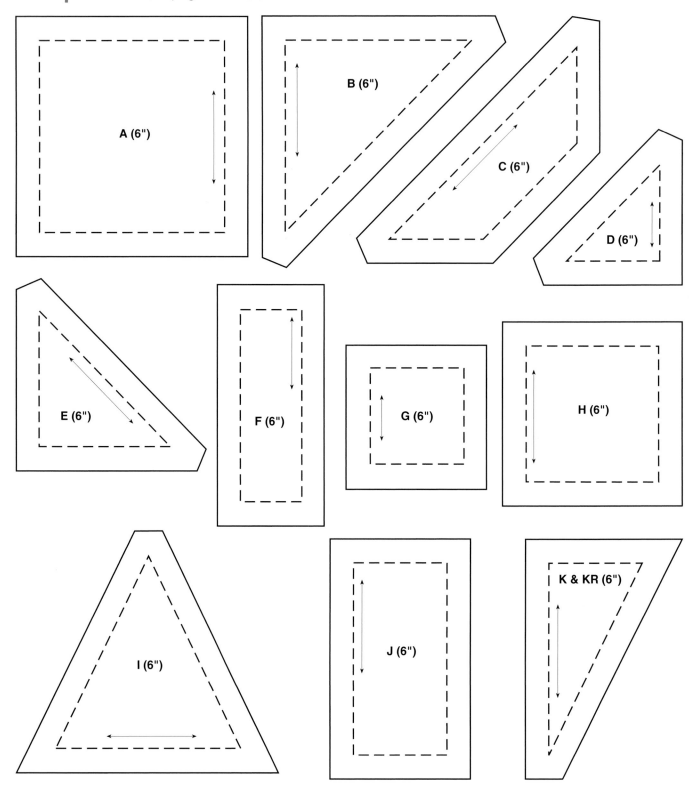

A (6")

B (6")

C (6")

D (6")

E (6")

F (6")

G (6")

H (6")

I (6")

J (6")

K & KR (6")

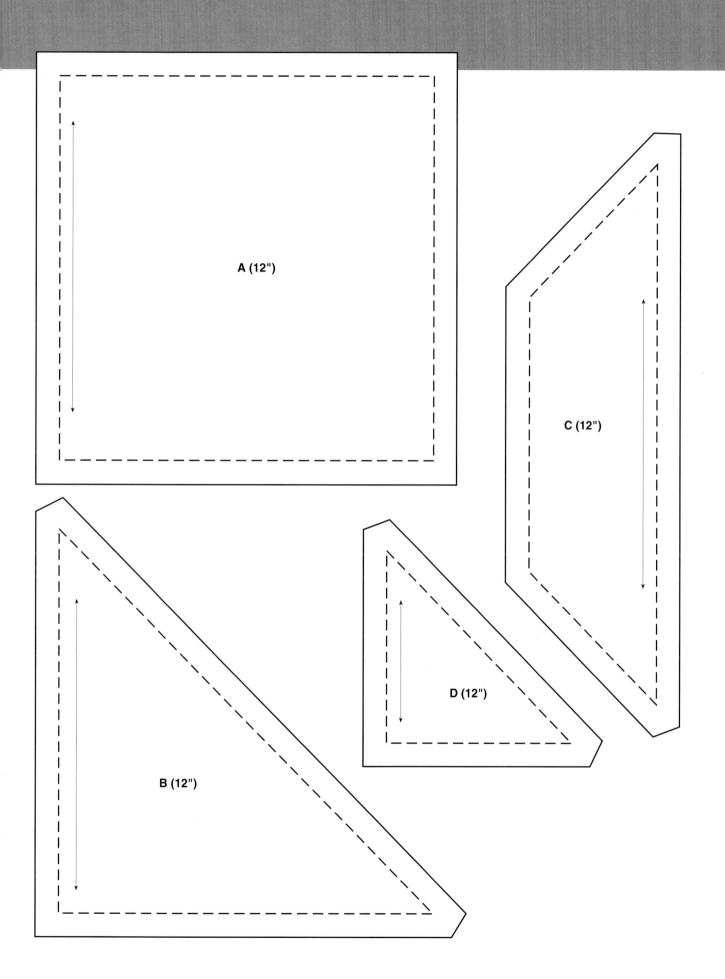

A (12")

C (12")

B (12")

D (12")

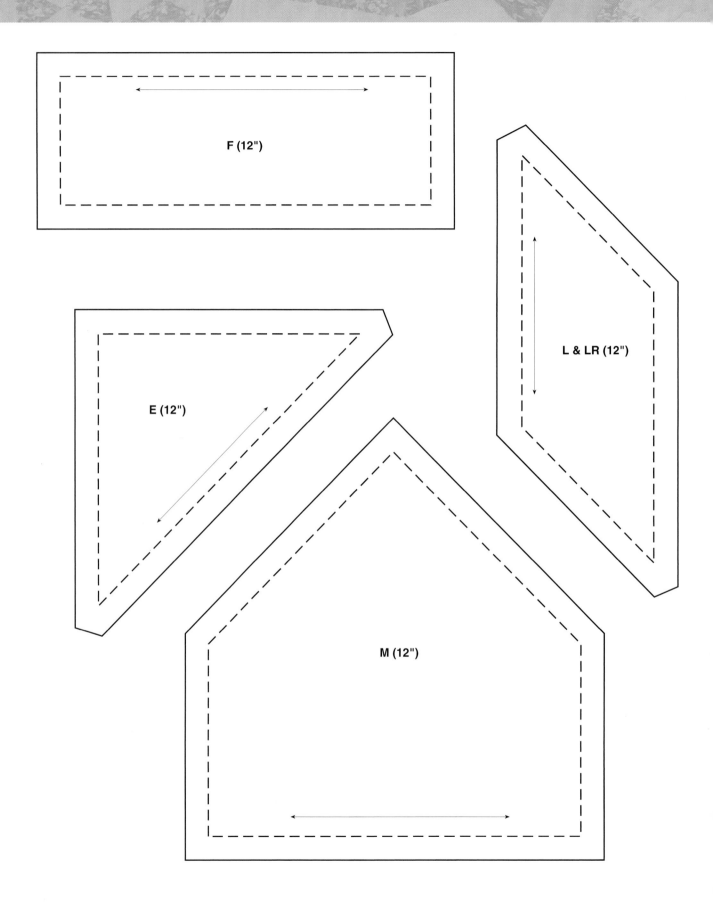

F (12")

L & LR (12")

E (12")

M (12")

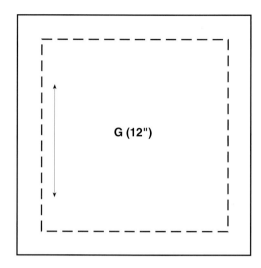

G (12")

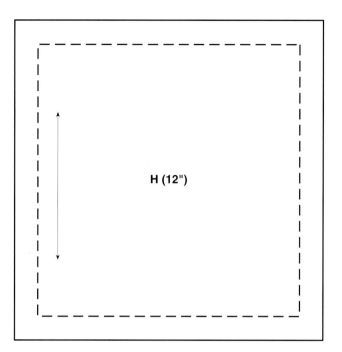

H (12")

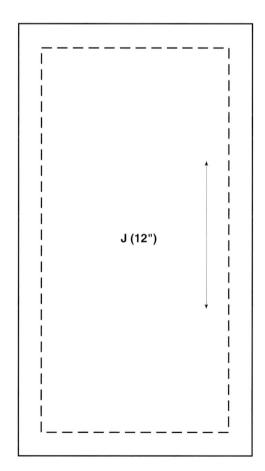

J (12")

Italian Flavors

These Nine-Patch pot holders will add a rainbow of rich flavors to your family's table.

Block Sizes
6" x 6" and 12" x 12"

Fabric
Scraps of the following fabrics: motif print, floral print, tan print, burgundy, white

Instructions
Note: *Use templates on pages 55–57. Prepare templates needed for your selected pot holder. Cut pieces for individual pot holder following the color diagram and/or the piecing instructions.*

Hourglass 2

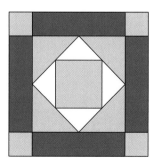
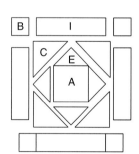

Hourglass 2
6" x 6" Block

Templates needed:
A, B, C, E & I

1. Referring to the Piecing Diagram, sew a white E to each side of a motif print A; add motif print C pieces to each side to complete the pieced center.

2. Arrange the pieced center in rows with motif print B and burgundy I pieces referring to the Piecing Diagram. Join to complete one block.

3. Finish pot holder as in General Instructions.

Housewife's Dream

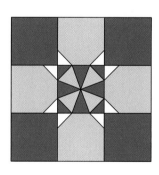
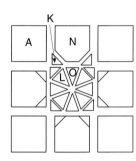

Housewife's Dream
6" x 6" Block

Templates needed:
A, K, L, N & O

1. Referring to the Piecing Diagram, sew a burgundy K to motif print L pieces.

2. Join K-L units with four burgundy O pieces to complete the block center.

3. Sew two white K pieces to a motif print N; repeat for four units.

4. Arrange the pieced units in rows with burgundy A squares referring to the Piecing Diagram. Join units in rows; join rows to complete one block.

5. Finish pot holder as in General Instructions.

Golden Gate

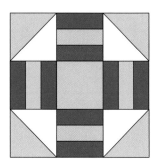

Golden Gate
6" x 6" Block

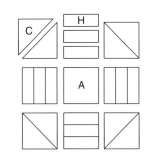

Templates needed:
A, C & H

1. Referring to the Piecing Diagram, sew a white C triangle to a motif print C triangle along the diagonal to complete a corner unit; repeat for four corner units.

2. Sew a motif print H piece between two burgundy H pieces to complete a side unit; repeat for four side units.

3. Arrange the pieced units in rows with one motif print A square referring to the Piecing Diagram. Join units in rows; join rows to complete one block.

4. Finish pot holder as in General Instructions.

Summer Winds

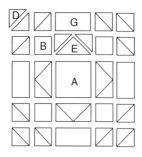

Summer Winds
12" x 12" Block

Templates needed:
A, B, D, E & G

1. Referring to the Piecing Diagram, sew a print D triangle to a burgundy D triangle along the diagonal; repeat for 12 units.

2. Join three D-D units with one floral print B square to complete a corner unit; repeat for four corner units.

3. Sew a tan print D triangle to adjacent short sides of a burgundy E triangle; repeat for four units. Sew a floral print G piece to each unit to complete a side unit; repeat for four side units.

4. Arrange pieced units in rows with the motif print A square referring to the Piecing Diagram. Join units in rows; join rows to complete one block.

5. Finish pot holder as in General Instructions. ■

Homey Comforts

Use a trendy birdhouse print in Nine-Patch designs to accent your kitchen decor.

Block Sizes
6" x 6" and 12" x 12"

Fabric
Scraps of the following fabrics: red print, blue print, cream, burgundy, bird print, white, motif print, floral print, red mottled

Instructions
Note: *Use templates on pages 55–57. Prepare templates needed for your selected pot holder. Cut pieces for individual pot holder following the color diagram and/or the piecing instructions.*

Ladies Aid Album

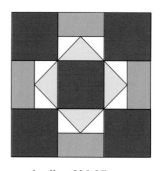

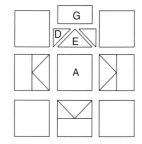

Ladies Aid Album
6" x 6" Block

Templates needed:
A, D, E & G

1. Referring to the Piecing Diagram, sew a white D triangle to adjacent short sides of a cream E triangle; sew a motif print G piece to the unit to complete one side unit. Repeat for four side units.

2. Arrange the pieced units in rows with five bird print A squares referring to the Piecing Diagram. Join units in rows; join rows to complete one block.

3. Finish pot holder as in General Instructions.

Weather Vane

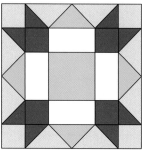
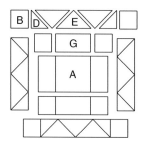

Weather Vane
6" x 6" Block

Templates needed:
A, B, D, E & G

1. Referring to the Piecing Diagram, sew a bird print G to opposite sides of a blue print A square. Sew a burgundy B square to each end of the remaining two G pieces; sew to remaining sides of the A square to complete the center unit.

2. Join two cream and one blue print E triangle to make a strip; sew a burgundy D triangle to each end to complete a side strip; repeat for four side strips.

3. Sew a side strip to opposite sides of the center unit. Sew a cream B square to each end of the remaining side strips. Sew these strips to the remaining sides of the pieced unit to complete one block.

4. Finish pot holder as in General Instructions.

Over & Under

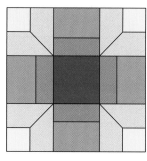
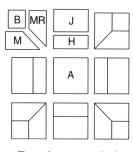

Over & Under
6" x 6" Block

Templates needed:
A, B, H, J, M & MR

1. Referring to the Piecing Diagram, sew a cream M to a cream MR; set in a floral print B square to make a corner unit. Repeat for four corner units.

2. Sew a red mottled H to a motif print J; repeat for four units.

3. Arrange the pieced units in rows with a motif print A square referring to the Piecing Diagram. Join units in rows; join rows to complete one block.

4. Finish pot holder as in General Instructions.

Kansas Star

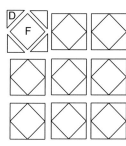

Kansas Star
12" x 12" Block

Templates needed:
D & F

1. Referring to the Piecing Diagram, sew a red print D triangle to each side of a motif print F square to complete one unit; repeat for nine units.

2. Arrange the units in rows referring to the Piecing Diagram. Join units in rows; join rows to complete one block.

3. Finish pot holder as in General Instructions. ∎

Templates (for pages 50–54)

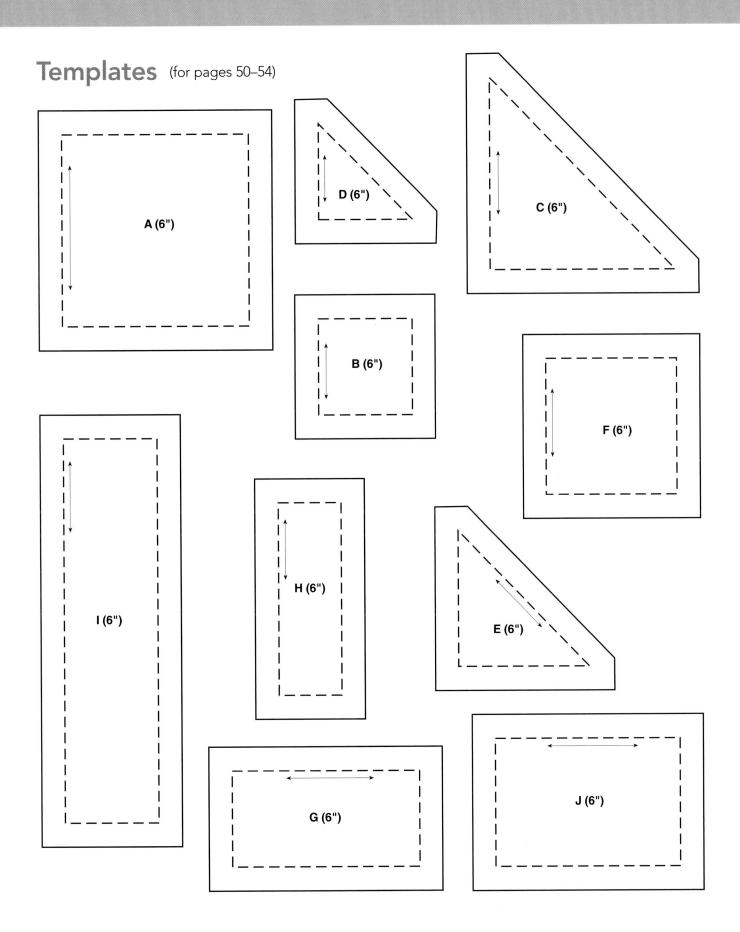

A (6")

D (6")

C (6")

B (6")

F (6")

I (6")

H (6")

E (6")

G (6")

J (6")

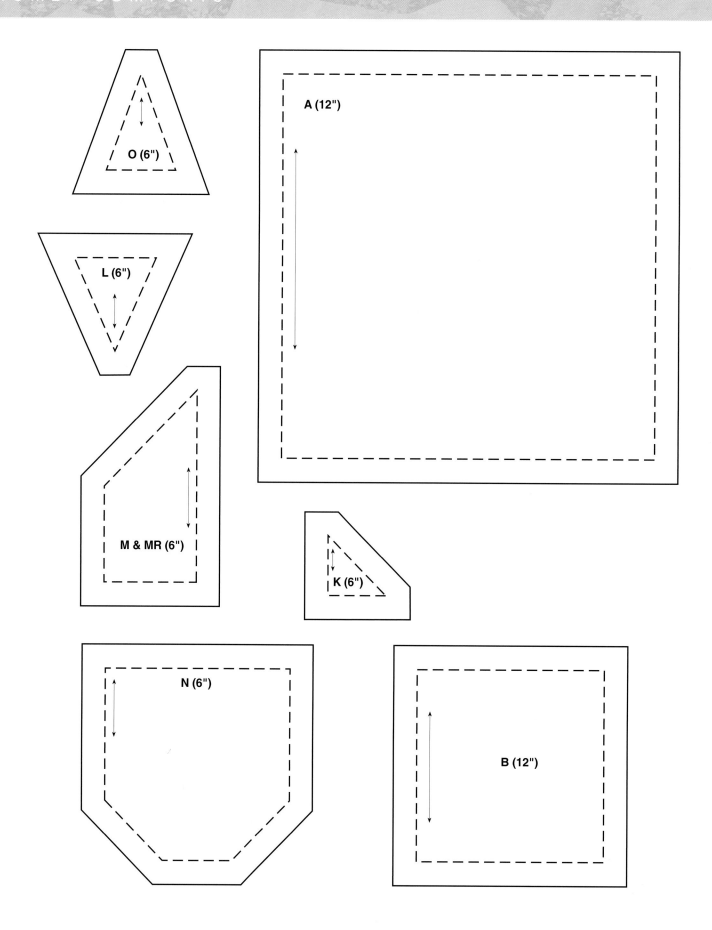

O (6")

L (6")

A (12")

M & MR (6")

K (6")

N (6")

B (12")

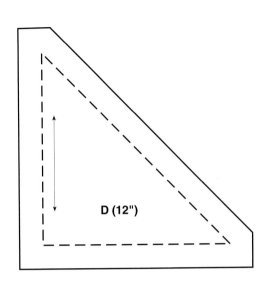

D (12")

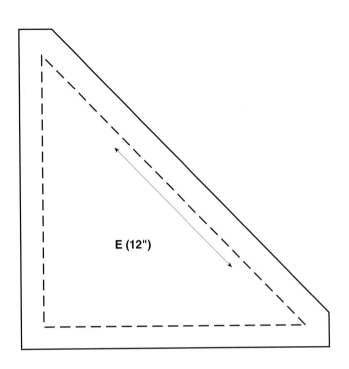

E (12")

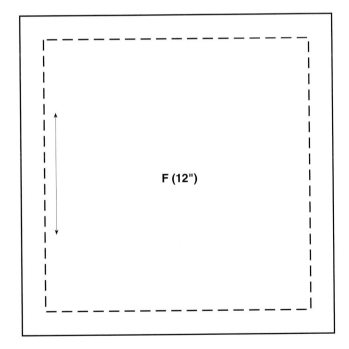

F (12")

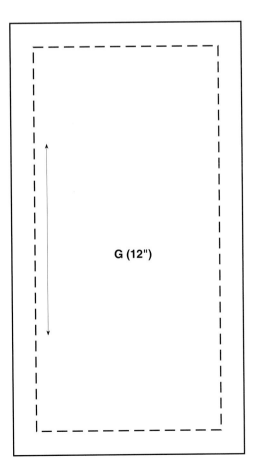

G (12")

Summer Sunshine

Pieced in the colors of sun and sky, these pot holders are as refreshing as a cool breeze on a warm summer day.

Block Size
6" x 6"

Fabric
Scraps of the following fabrics: blue, yellow, white, yellow floral, green, blue floral

Instructions
Note: Templates on page 81.

Twin Star

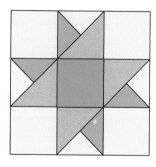
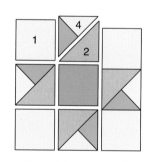

Twin Star
6" x 6" Block

Templates needed:
1, 2 & 4

1. Referring to the Piecing Diagram to piece one block, sew a blue 4 to a yellow 4 on the short sides; sew a yellow floral 2 to the joined unit to complete a side unit. Repeat for four side units.

2. Arrange the pieced units with one green and four yellow 1 squares in rows referring to the Piecing Diagram. Join units in rows; join rows to complete one block.

3. Finish pot holder as in General Instructions.

Cedars of Lebanon 1

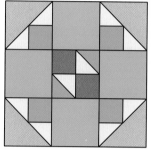
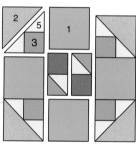

Cedars of Lebanon 1
6" x 6" Block

Templates needed:
1, 2, 3 & 5

1. Referring to the Piecing Diagram to piece one block, sew a yellow 5 to two adjacent sides of a green 3, sew a yellow floral 2 to the yellow side to complete one corner unit. Repeat for four corner units.

2. Sew a green 5 to a yellow 5 along the diagonal; repeat for two units. Join these two units with two blue floral 3 squares to complete the center unit.

3. Arrange the pieced units in rows with four blue 1 squares referring to the Piecing Diagram. Join units in rows; join rows to complete one block.

4. Finish pot holder as in General Instructions.

Crossroads

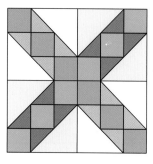

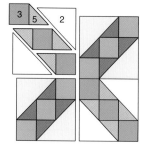

Crossroads
6" x 6" Block

Templates needed:
2, 3 & 5

1. Referring to the Piecing Diagram to piece one block, join four yellow floral 5 triangles with three green 3 squares and two white 2 triangles to make a corner unit; repeat for two corner units.

2. Join four blue floral 5 triangles with three blue 3 squares and two yellow 2 triangles to make a corner unit; repeat for two corner units.

3. Join the pieced units referring to the Piecing Diagram to complete one block.

4. Finish pot holder as in General Instructions.

Jacob's Ladder

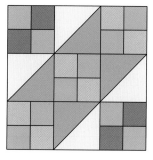

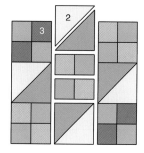

Jacob's Ladder
6" x 6" Block

Templates needed:
2 & 3

1. Referring to the Piecing Diagram to piece one block, join two blue and two blue floral 3 squares to make a Four-Patch corner unit; repeat for two corner units.

2. Join two blue and two yellow floral 3 squares to make a Four-Patch unit; repeat for one center unit and two corner units.

3. Sew a yellow 2 to a green 2 on the diagonal to make a side unit; repeat for four side units.

4. Arrange the pieced units in rows referring to the Piecing Diagram. Join units in rows; join rows to complete one block.

5. Finish pot holder as in General Instructions.

Love in a Mist

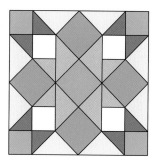

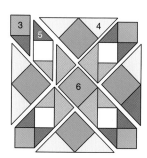

Love in a Mist
6" x 6" Block

Templates needed:
3, 4, 5 & 6

1. Referring to the Piecing Diagram to piece one block, sew a yellow floral and a blue floral 5 to a white 3; add a yellow floral 4 to one side. Sew a blue floral 5 to a blue 3 and sew to the opposite side to complete one corner unit; repeat for four corner units.

2. Join two units with a blue 6 for a center unit.

3. Sew a yellow 4 to two adjacent sides of a green 6 to complete a side unit; repeat for four side units.

4. Sew a corner unit between two side units; repeat. Sew these units to opposite sides of the previously pieced center unit to complete one block.

5. Finish pot holder as in General Instructions.

Saint Gregory's Cross

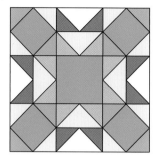

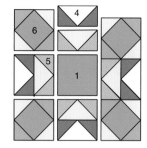

Saint Gregory's Cross
6" x 6" Block

Templates needed:
1, 4, 5 & 6

1. Referring to the Piecing Diagram to piece one block, sew two blue and two yellow 5 triangles to a green 6 to complete one corner unit; repeat for four corner units.

2. Sew a yellow floral 5 to two adjacent sides of a yellow 4; sew a blue floral 5 to two adjacent sides of a white 4. Join the two units to complete one side unit; repeat for four side units.

3. Arrange the pieced units with a green 1 square in rows referring to the Piecing Diagram. Join units in rows; join rows to complete one block.

4. Finish pot holder as in General Instructions.

Steps to the Altar

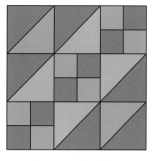

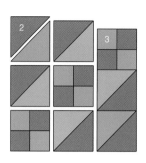

Steps to the Altar
6" x 6" Block

Templates needed:
2 & 3

1. Referring to the Piecing Diagram to piece one block, sew a green 2 to a blue floral 2 along the diagonal to make a corner unit; repeat for two corner units.

2. Sew a blue 2 to a blue floral 2 along the diagonal to complete a side unit; repeat for four side units.

3. Join two green and two blue floral 3 squares to make a Four-Patch unit; repeat for three Four-Patch units.

4. Arrange the pieced units referring to the Piecing Diagram. Join units in rows; join rows to complete one block.

5. Finish pot holder as in General Instructions. ■

Tangy Treats

Lip-smacking lemon, lime and orange add a tropical flair to everything you make.

Block Size
6" x 6"

Fabric
Scraps of the following fabrics: cream, orange, gold, green, green print, gold print

Instructions
Note: Templates on page 81.

Barbara Frietchie Star

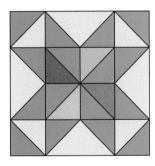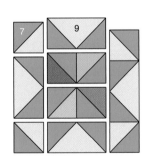

Barbara Frietchie Star
6" x 6" Block

Templates needed:
7 & 9

1. Referring to the Piecing Diagram to piece one block, sew a cream 7 to a green print 7 along the diagonal to complete a corner unit; repeat for four corner units.

2. Sew an orange, gold, gold print and green 7 to a green print 7 along the diagonal to complete four units. Join four units to complete a pinwheel center.

3. Sew a green print 7 to two adjacent sides of a cream 9 to complete one side unit; repeat for four side units.

4. Arrange the pieced units in rows referring to the Piecing Diagram. Join units in rows; join rows to complete one block.

5. Finish pot holder as in General Instructions.

Broken Dishes

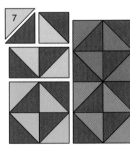

Broken Dishes
6" x 6" Block

Template needed:
7

1. Referring to the Piecing Diagram to piece one block, sew the orange, gold, gold print and green 7's to the green print 7's along the diagonals.

2. Arrange four same-color units to make a block quarter; join units to complete one quarter. Repeat for four quarters. Join the quarters to complete one block.

3. Finish pot holder as in General Instructions.

Pinwheel 2

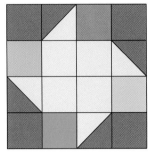

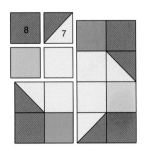

Pinwheel 2
6" x 6" Block

Templates needed:
7 & 8

1. Referring to the Piecing Diagram to piece one block, sew a cream 7 to an orange 7 along the diagonal; repeat for four units.

2. Arrange the pieced units in quarters with one each orange and cream 8 squares and one each green, gold, gold print or green print 8 squares referring to the Piecing Diagram. Join quarter units to complete one block.

3. Finish pot holder as in General Instructions.

Road to Oklahoma

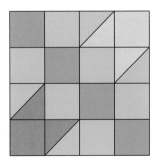
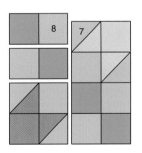

Road To Oklahoma
6" x 6" Block

Templates needed:
7 & 8

1. Referring to the Piecing Diagram to piece one block, sew a gold 7 to a green 7 along the diagonal; repeat for two units. Sew a 7 unit to a gold and a green 8 square. Join the 7-8 units to make a block quarter.

2. Sew a gold print 7 to a green 7 along the

diagonal; repeat for two units. Sew a 7 unit to a green and a gold print 8 square. Join the 7-8 units to make a block quarter.

3. Join two green and two green print 8 squares to complete a Four-Patch block quarter; repeat for two quarters.

4. Join the block quarters to complete one block.

5. Finish pot holder as in General Instructions.

Unknown Four-Patch

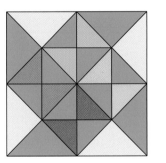
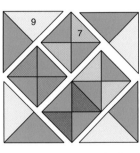

Unknown Four-Patch
6" x 6" Block

Templates needed:
7 & 9

1. Referring to the Piecing Diagram to piece one block, join two green and two green print 7's to make a square unit. Join two gold and two green print 7's to make a square unit. Join two orange and two green print 7's to make a square unit. Join two gold print and two green print 7's to make a square unit. Join four square units to create the pinwheel center.

2. Sew a cream 9 to a green print 9 on the short sides to complete a corner unit; repeat for four corner units.

3. Sew a corner unit to each side of the center unit to complete one block.

4. Finish pot holder as in General Instructions.

Windmill

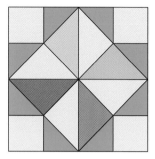 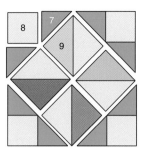

Windmill
6" x 6" Block

Templates needed:
7, 8 & 9

1. Referring to the Piecing Diagram to piece one block, sew the orange, gold, gold print and green 9's to the cream 9's on the diagonal. Join the units to complete the pinwheel center unit.

2. Sew a green print 7 to two adjacent sides of a cream 8 to complete a corner unit; repeat for four corner units.

3. Sew a corner unit to each side of the center unit to complete one block.

4. Finish pot holder as in General Instructions.

X Quartet

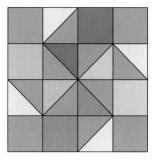 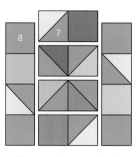

X Quartet
6" x 6" Block

Templates needed:
7 & 8

1. Referring to the Piecing Diagram to piece one block, sew a cream 7 to a green print 7 along the diagonal; repeat for four units.

2. Sew an orange, green, gold and gold print 7's to green print 7's along the diagonals to make four units. Join the units to make the pinwheel center unit.

3. Arrange the pieced units in rows with four green print and one each orange, green, gold and gold print 8 squares referring to the Piecing Diagram. Join units in rows; join rows to complete one block.

4. Finish pot holder as in General Instructions. ■

Hot & Sassy

Get energized with the bright, bold colors in these small projects.

Block Size
6" x 6"

Fabric
Scraps of the following fabrics: lime, purple, pink, orange, turquoise, yellow

Instructions
Note: *Templates on page 81.*

Yankee Puzzle

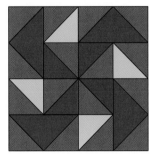 

Yankee Puzzle
6" x 6" Block

Templates needed:
7 & 9

1. Referring to the Piecing Diagram to piece one block, sew a purple 7 to a lime 7 along the diagonal; repeat for four units. Sew a purple 7 to a pink 7 along the diagonal; repeat for four units.

2. Sew a purple 7 to two adjacent sides of a pink 9; repeat for four units.

3. Join two 7 units with a 7-9 unit to complete one quarter block; repeat for four quarter blocks.

4. Join the quarter blocks to complete one block.

5. Finish pot holder as in General Instructions.

Brown Goose

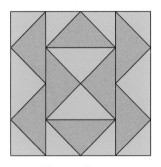 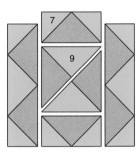

Brown Goose
6" x 6" Block

Templates needed:
7 & 9

1. Referring to the Piecing Diagram to piece one block, sew a lime 7 to two adjacent short sides of an orange 9; repeat.

2. Join two lime and two orange 9 triangles to complete the block center; sew a 7-9 unit to two opposite lime sides to complete the center unit.

3. Join one lime and two orange 9 triangles with two lime 7 triangles to complete a long side unit; repeat for two long side units.

4. Sew a long side unit to opposite sides of the pieced center unit to complete one block.

5. Finish pot holder as in General Instructions.

Old Gray Goose

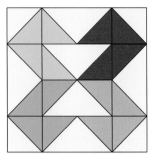 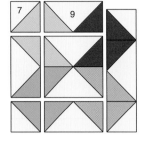

Old Gray Goose
6" x 6" Block

Templates needed:
7 & 9

1. Referring to the Piecing Diagram to piece one block, sew a lime, pink, orange and turquoise 7 to a yellow 7 along the diagonal to complete four corner units.

2. Sew an orange and a turquoise 7 to two adjacent sides of a yellow 9; repeat for two units. Sew a pink and a lime 7 to two adjacent sides of a yellow 9; repeat for two units. Sew an orange and a pink 7 to two adjacent sides of a yellow 9. Sew a lime and a turquoise 7 to two adjacent sides of a yellow 9. Join two 7-9 units referring to the Piecing Diagram to complete the block center.

3. Sew a 7-9 unit to opposite sides of the block center. Sew a corner unit to each end of the remaining 7-9 units with yellow sides on the outside. Sew these units to the previously pieced unit to complete one block.

4. Finish pot holder as in General Instructions.

Spider 1

1. Referring to the Piecing Diagram to piece one block, sew the purple, pink, orange and turquoise 7's to the lime 7's along the diagonal; repeat for 4 units of each color combination.

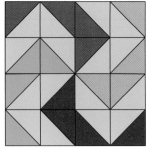 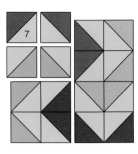

Spider 1
6" x 6" Block

Template needed:
7

2. Arrange the units in rows referring to the Piecing Diagram to complete the design. Join units in rows; join rows to complete one block.

3. Finish pot holder as in General Instructions.

Wild Duck

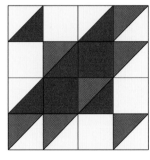 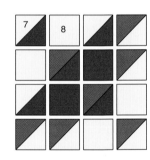

Wild Duck
6" x 6" Block

Templates needed:
7 & 8

1. Referring to the Piecing Diagram to piece one block, sew a yellow 7 to a pink 7 along the diagonal; repeat for three units. Sew a yellow 7 to a purple 7 along the diagonal; repeat for five units. Sew a pink 7 to a purple 7 along the diagonal repeat for two units.

2. Arrange the pieced units in rows with four yellow and two pink 8 squares referring to the Piecing Diagram. Join units in rows; join rows to complete one block.

3. Finish pot holder as in General Instructions.

Indian Star

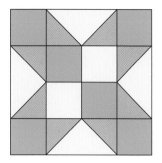

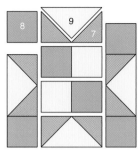

Indian Star
6" x 6" Block

Templates needed:
7, 8 & 9

1. Referring to the Piecing Diagram to piece one block, join two yellow and two turquoise 8 squares to make the center Four-Patch unit.

2. Sew an orange 7 to two adjacent sides of a yellow 9; repeat for four units. Sew a unit to two opposite sides of the center unit.

3. Sew a turquoise 8 to each end of the remaining two 7-9 units; sew these units to the remaining sides of the center unit to complete one block.

4. Finish pot holder as in General Instructions.

Balkan Puzzle

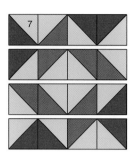

Balkan Puzzle
6" x 6" Block

Template needed:
7

1. Referring to the Piecing Diagram to piece one block, sew the pink and purple 7's to the lime 7's to complete 16 units.

2. Arrange the pieced units in rows referring to the Piecing Diagram. Join units in rows; join rows to complete one block.

3. Finish pot holder as in General Instructions. ■

These timeless projects satisfy like your favorite comfort foods.

Block Size
6" x 6"

Fabric
Scraps of the following fabrics: pink, pink print, rose floral, black floral

Instructions
Note: Templates on page 81.

Darting Birds

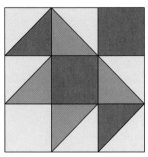

Darting Birds
6" x 6" Block

Templates needed:
1 & 2

1. Referring to the Piecing Diagram to piece one block, sew a pink print 2 to a black floral 2 along the diagonal; repeat for two units.

2. Sew a pink print 2 to a rose floral 2 along the diagonal; repeat for four units.

3. Arrange the pieced units in rows with one pink print and two black floral 1 squares referring to the Piecing Diagram. Join units in rows; join rows to complete one block.

4. Finish pot holder as in General Instructions.

Flying Crow

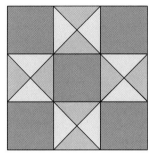
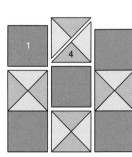

Flying Crow
6" x 6" Block

Templates needed:
1 & 4

1. Referring to the Piecing Diagram to piece one block, join two pink and two pink print 4 triangles to complete a side unit; repeat for four side units.

2. Arrange the side units in rows with five rose floral 1 squares referring to the Piecing Diagram. Join units in rows; join rows to complete one block.

3. Finish pot holder as in General Instructions.

Puss in the Corner 1

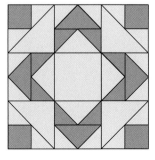
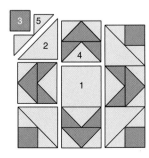

Puss in the Corner 1
6" x 6" Block

Templates needed:
1, 2, 3, 4 & 5

1. Referring to the Piecing Diagram to piece one block, sew a pink print 5 to two adjacent sides of a rose floral 3; add a pink print 2 on the long side to complete a corner unit. Repeat for four corner units.

2. Sew a rose floral 5 to two adjacent sides of a pink print 4 and a pink print 5 to two adjacent sides of a rose floral 4; join the two pieced units to complete a side unit. Repeat for four side units.

3. Arrange the pieced units in rows with a pink print 1 square referring to the Piecing Diagram. Join units in rows; join rows to complete one block.

4. Finish pot holder as in General Instructions.

Buckwheat

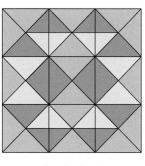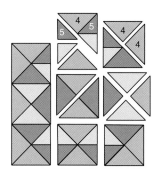

Buckwheat
6" x 6" Block

Templates needed:
4 & 5

1. Referring to the Piecing Diagram to piece one block, sew a rose floral 5 to a pink print 5; repeat for eight units. Sew a rose floral 4 to the pink print side of four pieced 5-5 units.

2. Sew a pink 4 to a pink 4; repeat for four units. Sew a 4-4 unit to a 4-5 unit to complete a corner unit; repeat for four corner units.

3. Sew a pink print 4 to a pink 4 and a pink print 4 to a rose floral 4; repeat for two of each unit. Join

one of each unit to complete a side unit. Repeat for two side units.

4. Sew a pink 4 to a rose floral 4; repeat for two units. Join these two units to make one center unit.

5. Sew a pink 4 to a rose floral/pink print 5-5 unit; repeat for four units. Join two 4-5 units to make top and bottom units.

6. Arrange units in rows and join to complete one block.

7. Finish pot holder as in General Instructions.

Cobweb

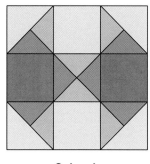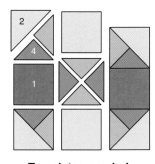

Cobweb
6" x 6" Block

Templates needed:
1, 2 & 4

1. Referring to the Piecing Diagram to piece one block, sew a pink 4 to a rose floral 4; sew this unit to a pink print 2. Repeat for four units.

2. Sew a pink 4 to a rose floral 4; repeat for two units. Join the two units to complete one center unit.

3. Join the pieced center and corner units with two black floral and two pink print 1 pieces to make rows; join rows to complete one block.

4. Finish pot holder as in General Instructions.

Lightning in the Hills

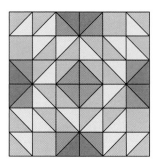

Lightning in the Hills
6" x 6" Block

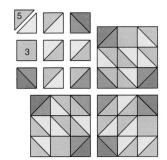

Templates needed:
3 & 5

1. Referring to the Piecing Diagram to piece one block, sew a pink 5 to a pink print 5 along the diagonal; repeat for 20 units.

2. Sew a rose floral 5 to a black floral 5 along the diagonal; repeat for eight units.

3. Sew a pink 5 to a rose floral 5 along the diagonal; repeat for four units.

4. Arrange the pieced units in rows with four pink 3 pieces referring to the Piecing Diagram. Join units in rows; join rows to complete one block.

5. Finish pot holder as in General Instructions. ■

Baking Pleasure

Sweet treats from your kitchen bring satisfied smiles all around.

Block Size
6" x 6"

Fabric
Scraps of the following fabrics: green, blue, pink, burgundy print, floral print

Instructions
Note: *Templates on page 81.*

Four Crowns

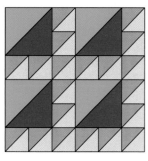 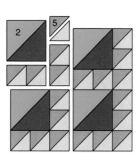

Four Crowns
6" x 6" Block

Templates needed:
2 & 5

1. Referring to the Piecing Diagram to piece one block, sew a pink 5 to a blue 5 along the diagonal; repeat for 5 units. Join two units to make a row; join three units to make a row.

2. Sew a green 2 to a burgundy print 2 along the diagonal.

3. Sew the two- and three-unit 5 rows with the 2 unit to complete one quarter unit; repeat for four quarter units.

4. Join the quarter units to complete one block.

5. Finish pot holder as in General Instructions.

Road to the White House

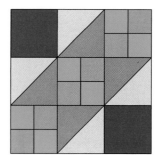 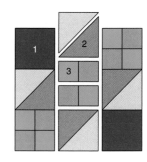

Road to the White House
6" x 6" Block

Templates needed:
1, 2 & 3

1. Referring to the Piecing Diagram to piece one block, join two green and two blue 3 squares to make a Four-Patch unit; repeat for three units.

2. Sew a pink 2 to a floral print 2 along the diagonal to make a side unit; repeat for four side units.

3. Arrange the pieced units in rows with two burgundy print 1 squares referring to the Piecing Diagram. Join units in rows; join rows to complete one block.

4. Finish pot holder as in General Instructions.

Square & Half-Square

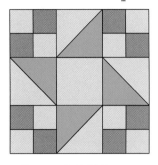

Square & Half-Square
6" x 6" Block

Templates needed:
1, 2 & 3

1. Referring to the Piecing Diagram to piece one block, join two pink and two floral print 3 squares to make a Four-Patch corner unit; repeat for four corner units.

2. Sew a pink 2 to a green 2 along the diagonal to make one side unit; repeat for four side units.

3. Arrange the pieced units in rows with one pink 1 square referring to the Piecing Diagram. Join units in rows; join rows to complete one block.

4. Finish pot holder as in General Instructions.

Mystery Flower Garden

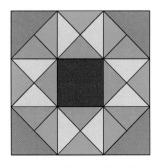
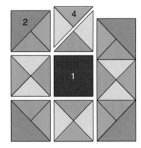

Mystery Flower Garden
6" x 6" Block

Templates needed:
1, 2 & 4

1. Referring to the Piecing Diagram to piece one block, join one green, one blue and two pink 4 triangles to complete one side unit; repeat for four side units.

2. Join one green and one blue 4 with a floral print 2 to complete one corner unit; repeat for four corner units.

3. Arrange the pieced units in rows with the burgundy print 1 square referring to the Piecing Diagram. Join units in rows; join rows to complete one block.

4. Finish pot holder as in General Instructions.

Practical Orchard

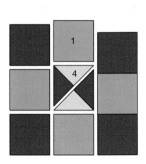

Practical Orchard
6" x 6" Block

Templates needed:
1 & 4

1. Referring to the Piecing Diagram to piece one block, join two pink and two burgundy print 4 triangles to complete the center unit.

2. Arrange the center unit in rows with four blue and four burgundy print 1 squares referring to the Piecing Diagram. Join units in rows; join rows to complete one block.

3. Finish pot holder as in General Instructions.

Tulip Ladyfingers

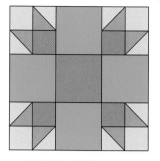

Tulip Ladyfingers
6" x 6" Block

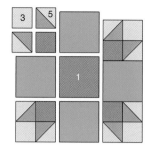

Templates needed:
1, 3 & 5

1. Referring to the Piecing Diagram to piece one block, sew a pink 5 to a blue 5 along the diagonal; repeat for eight units.

2. Join two units with one pink and one floral print 3 to complete one corner unit; repeat for four corner units.

3. Arrange the pieced units in rows with one floral print and four green 1 squares referring to the Piecing Diagram. Join units in rows; join rows to complete one block.

4. Finish pot holder as in General Instructions. ■

Berry Burst

As luscious as fresh berries and cream, these projects will whet your appetite.

Block Size
6" x 6"

Fabric
Scraps of the following fabrics: lavender, purple, pink print, lavender print, purple print

Instructions
Note: Templates on page 81.

Path Through the Woods

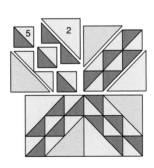

Path Through the Woods
6" x 6" Block

Templates needed:
2 & 5

1. Referring to the Piecing Diagram to piece one block, sew a lavender 5 to a purple 5 along the diagonal; repeat for 12 units.

2. Join three pieced units with two lavender and two purple 5 pieces to make one pieced strip referring to the Piecing Diagram; repeat for four pieced strips.

3. Sew a pink print 2 to one side of one pieced unit and a lavender 2 to the opposite side; repeat for four units.

4. Join the four pieced units referring to the Piecing Diagram to complete one block.

5. Finish pot holder as in General Instructions.

Braced Star

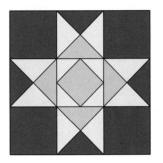
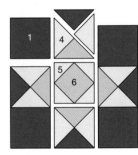

Braced Star
6" x 6" Block

Templates needed:
1, 4, 5 & 6

1. Referring to the Piecing Diagram to piece one block, join two lavender and one each purple print and lavender print 4 triangles to make a side unit; repeat for four units.

2. Sew a lavender 5 to each side of a lavender print 6 to complete the center unit.

3. Arrange the units with four purple print 1 squares in rows referring to the Piecing Diagram. Join units in rows; join rows to complete one block.

4. Finish pot holder as in General Instructions.

Card Basket

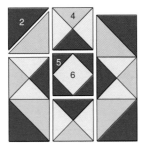

Card Basket
6" x 6" Block

Templates needed:
2, 4, 5 & 6

1. Referring to the Piecing Diagram to piece one block, sew a purple print 2 to a lavender print 2 along the diagonal to make a corner unit; repeat for four corner units.

2. Join two lavender, one lavender print and one purple print 4 triangles to complete one side unit; repeat for four side units.

3. Sew a purple print 5 to each side of a lavender 6 to complete the center unit.

4. Arrange the units in rows referring to the Piecing Diagram. Join units in rows; join rows to complete one block.

5. Finish pot holder as in General Instructions.

Eccentric Star

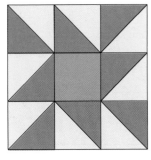

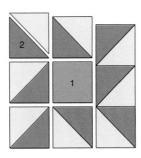

Eccentric Star
6" x 6" Block

Templates needed:
1 & 2

1. Referring to the Piecing Diagram to piece one block, sew a lavender 2 to a purple 2 along the diagonal; repeat for eight units.

2. Arrange the pieced units with one print 1 square in rows referring to the Piecing Diagram. Join units in rows; join rows to complete one block.

3. Finish pot holder as in General Instructions.

Ribbon Quilt

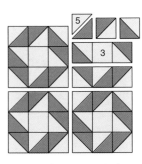

Ribbon Quilt
6" x 6" Block

Templates needed:
3 & 5

1. Referring to the Piecing Diagram to piece one block, sew a lavender 5 to a purple 5 along the diagonal; repeat for 32 units.

2. Arrange the pieced units in rows with lavender 3 squares to form four corner units; join in rows. Join corner units to complete one block.

3. Finish pot holder as in General Instructions. ◼

Templates (for pages 58–80)

1

2

3

4

5

6

7

8

9

General Instructions for Appliqué

1. Prepare templates for each appliqué shape. Transfer cutting instructions for the chosen project or projects to templates.

2. Cut shapes as indicated on pattern piece for number and fabric color, adding a ¼" seam allowance to each piece and reversing template to trace on the wrong side of the fabric. Cut an identical shape from medium-weight fusible interfacing for each fabric piece needed.

3. Place appliqué pieces right sides together with the fusible side of the medium-weight fusible interfacing pieces; stitch around seam allowance, using all-purpose thread to match fabric. Clip curves and trim points to a ⅛" seam allowance.

4. Cut a slit in the interfacing side of the stitched units. Turn each unit right side out through the slit using a knitting needle, pencil with broken lead or stylet to smooth seams and points. **Note:** *Fusible side of interfacing should be on the outside.*

5. Draw any detail lines on motifs using a water-erasable fabric marker or pencil referring to the pattern for placement.

6. Using drawings provided with each project, arrange the appliqué shapes on the background fabrics in numerical order. Iron in place with a medium-hot iron.

7. Cut a piece of fabric stabilizer to fit under the appliqué area or areas. Pin to the wrong side of the appliqué area or areas.

8. Using clear nylon monofilament in the top of the machine and all-purpose thread in the bobbin and a machine blind-hem stitch, stitch edge of shapes in place.

9. Remove fabric stabilizer when all stitching is complete referring to manufacturer's instructions.

Making Yo-Yos

1. Using circle pattern for yo-yo given on page 93, cut as directed in individual pattern instructions for color and number to cut.

2. Turn under the edge of circle ¼" all around and hand-stitch using a long gathering stitch. Pull the thread tightly to gather the outside edges to the center to make a yo-yo as shown in Figure 1.

3. Make a knot to tie off and hold gathering stitches; cut thread. Flatten yo-yo between your fingers to form a small, round circle for holly berries or poinsettia centers.

Figure 1
Pull threads to gather to make a yo-yo.

Rounding Corners

1. Make template for rounded corner using pattern given.

2. Use template to round three corners of pot holder top, backing and batting referring to the project Placement Diagram for positioning of round corners. ■

Rounded Corner Pattern

Lucky Shamrock

Add the luck of the Irish to your kitchen.

Block Size
8" x 8"

Materials
- One 9" x 9" square each light, medium and dark green prints
- 1 square each backing and cotton batting 8½" x 8½"
- ⅛ yard medium-weight fusible interfacing
- ⅛ yard fabric stabilizer
- 1⅛ yards self-made or purchased green bias binding

Instructions

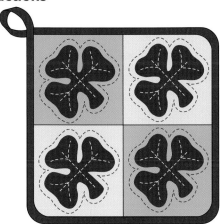

Lucky Shamrock
Placement Diagram
8" x 8"

1. Prepare template for shamrock using pattern piece given; cut as directed on the piece.

2. Cut two squares each 4½" x 4½" light and medium green prints.

3. Join the squares to complete the pieced top referring to the Placement Diagram for positioning of squares.

4. Round corners on pieced square using the template provided in the General Instructions for Appliqué on page 82.

5. Prepare shamrock pieces for appliqué and appliqué shamrocks in place referring to the General Instructions for Appliqué on page 82.

6. Prepare for quilting and quilt as desired.

7. Bind edges and make a hanging loop to finish. ■

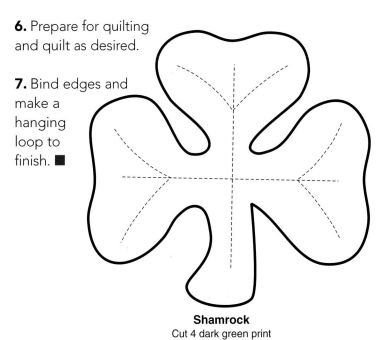

Shamrock
Cut 4 dark green print

Spring Tulips

Swing into spring with a tulip-motif pot holder.

Block Size
8½" x 8½"

Materials
- Scraps red, yellow and green prints
- ⅛ yard blue print
- ¼ yard white solid
- 1 square each backing and cotton batting 9" x 9"
- ⅛ yard medium-weight fusible interfacing
- ⅛ yard fabric stabilizer
- 1⅛ yards self-made or purchased blue bias binding

Instructions

Spring Tulips
Placement Diagram
8¹/₂" x 8¹/₂"

1. Prepare templates for tulip motif using pattern given; cut as directed on the pattern.

2. Cut one square blue print and four squares white solid 2½" x 2½" for A.

3. Cut one strip each blue print and white solid 1½" x 13". Sew the strips together along length with right sides together; press seams toward blue print strip.

4. Subcut strip set into 1½" segments; you will need eight segments. Join two segments as shown in Figure 1 to make a Four-Patch unit; repeat for four units.

Figure 1
Join 2 segments to
make a Four-Patch unit.

5. Join the A squares with the Four-Patch units in rows as shown in Figure 2; join rows to complete an Irish Chain unit. Press seams in one direction.

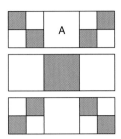

Figure 2
Join the A squares with the
Four-Patch units in rows.

6. Cut two squares white solid 5⅛" x 5⅛"; cut each square on one diagonal to make triangles. Sew a triangle to each side of the Irish Chain unit; press seams away from the triangles.

7. Round corners on pieced square using template provided in the General Instructions for Appliqué on page 82.

8. Prepare tulip motif pieces for appliqué and appliqué in place referring to the General Instructions for Appliqué on page 82.

9. Prepare for quilting and quilt as desired.

10. Bind edges and make a hanging loop. ■

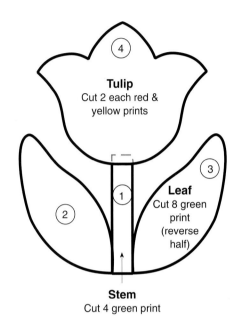

Tulip
Cut 2 each red &
yellow prints

Leaf
Cut 8 green
print
(reverse
half)

Stem
Cut 4 green print

Apples & Cherries

Apples and cherries bring cheer to your kitchen.

Block Size
8" x 8"

Materials
- ⅓ yard white solid
- ⅜ yard blue-and-white print
- ¾ yard blue dot
- Scraps red dot, red solid, green solid and green print
- 2 squares batting 8½" x 8½"
- 6" x 6" square fabric stabilizer
- 8" x 8" square medium-weight fusible interfacing
- 1 spool each brown and green rayon thread

Instructions

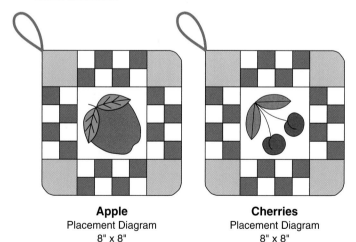

Apple
Placement Diagram
8" x 8"

Cherries
Placement Diagram
8" x 8"

1. Cut two squares white solid 4½" x 4½".

2. Prepare appliqué pieces for one each cherry and apple motif with leaves referring to patterns and General Instructions for Appliqué on page 82.

3. Center a cherry motif on one 4½" x 4½" white square and an apple motif on the other. Appliqué in place. Referring to the Placement Diagram, draw cherry stems and apple stems on background with a water-soluble pen. Machine-zigzag apple stem with brown rayon thread and cherry stems with green rayon thread.

4. Cut one strip each blue dot and white solid 1½" by fabric width on a cutting mat using a rotary cutter and ruler.

5. Sew strips together along length; press seam toward blue dot.

6. Cut stitched strip into 1½" segments as shown in Figure 1; repeat across strip.

Figure 1
Cut stitched strip into 1½" segments.

7. Construct two checkerboard strips using four segments in each strip as shown in Figure 2; repeat for eight checkerboard strips (four for each pot holder).

Figure 2
Join 4 segments to make a checkerboard strip.

8. Cut eight squares blue-and-white print 2½" x 2½". Sew a checkerboard strip between two squares as shown in Figure 3; repeat for four units.

2½" x 2½"

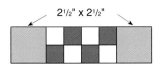

Figure 3
Sew a square to each side of a checkerboard strip.

9. Sew a checkerboard strip to opposite sides of each appliquéd square as shown in Figure 4.

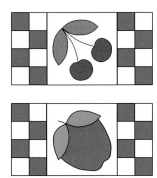

Figure 4
Sew a checkerboard strip to each side of each appliquéd square.

10. Join the pieced sections as shown in Figure 5 to complete pot holder tops.

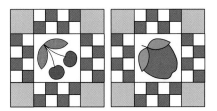

Figure 5
Join pieced sections as shown.

11. Round three corners on each pot holder using pattern provided in the General Instructions for Appliqué on page 82.

12. Prepare for quilting and quilt as desired.

13. Bind edges and make hanging loop. ■

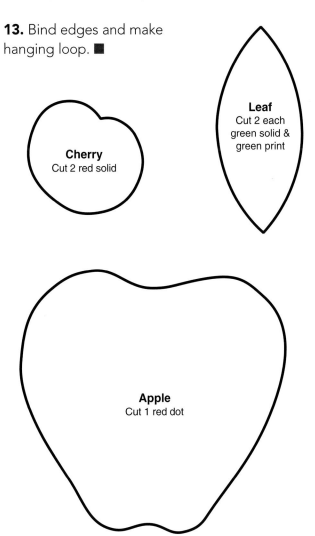

Leaf
Cut 2 each
green solid &
green print

Cherry
Cut 2 red solid

Apple
Cut 1 red dot

Fall Harvest

This pot holder is pretty enough to use as a decoration.

Block Size
9" x 9"

Materials
- Scraps dark green and corn prints; gold and green mottleds and coral and orange solids
- Fat eight each rose and tan prints and brown solid
- ⅓ yard muslin
- Batting 10" x 10"
- ⅛ yard medium-weight fusible interfacing
- 7" x 7" square fabric stabilizer

Instructions

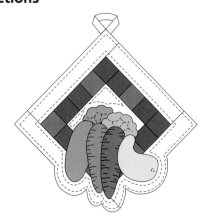

Fall Harvest
Placement Diagram
9" x 9"

1. Prepare templates for small corn, small and medium carrots, small squash and carrot leaves using patterns given. Referring to the General Instructions for Appliqué on page 82, prepare fabric patches for design as directed on each piece; set aside.

2. Cut five squares each rose and tan scraps and six squares brown scrap 1¾" x 1¾". Prepare two border strips each with three squares and five squares referring to Figure 1.

3 squares

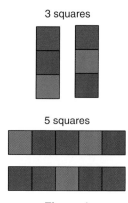

5 squares

Figure 1
Prepare border strips as shown.

3. Cut a muslin square 4¼" x 4¼". Referring to Figure 2, sew the shorter border strips to the two opposite sides; press seams toward strips. Sew the longer border strips to the remaining sides; press seams toward strips.

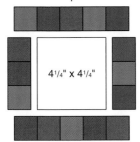

Figure 2
Sew strips to the 4¼" x 4¼"
square as shown.

4. Cut one strip muslin 1½" x 6¾" and sew to the top right end of the bordered pot holder as shown in Figure 3; press seam toward strip. Cut another strip muslin 1½" x 7¾"; sew to the top left end. Press seam toward strip. Cut another strip muslin 3" x 7¾"; sew to the bottom right end. Press seam toward strip. Cut the final strip 3" x 10¼" and sew to the bottom left end of the bordered pot holder; press seam toward strip.

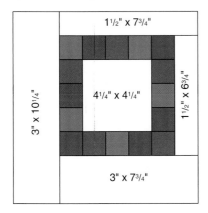

Figure 3
Sew muslin strips to bordered pot
holder in the order shown.

5. Prepare each appliqué motif referring to the General Instructions for Appliqué on page 82. Layer and pin prepared vegetable pieces in numerical order on corner of the wider muslin strips referring to Figure 4; fuse in place.

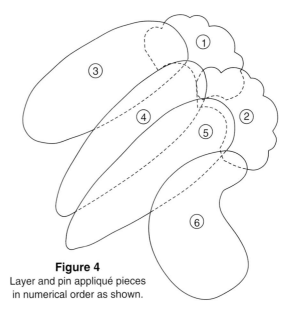

Figure 4
Layer and pin appliqué pieces
in numerical order as shown.

6. Machine-appliqué each shape in place referring to the General Instructions for Appliqué.

7. Measure and mark lines 1¼" from edge of appliqué shapes and 1½" from edge of pieced border; cut on marked lines.

8. Cut a 1¾" x 3½" strip muslin. Fold in half along length with right sides together; stitch. Turn right side out. Pin ends to the sides at corner opposite appliquéd motif as shown in Figure 5.

Figure 5
Pin loop piece at sides
on corner as shown.

9. Cut a piece of muslin 10" x 10" for backing. Using cut pot holder as a pattern, cut batting and muslin to the same shape. Pin batting to wrong side of pot holder and backing right sides together with pot holder top. Stitch all around using a ¼" seam allowance, leaving a 4" opening on one side. Turn right side out through opening. Smooth curves and seams; press. Hand-stitch opening closed.

10. Quilt as desired. ■

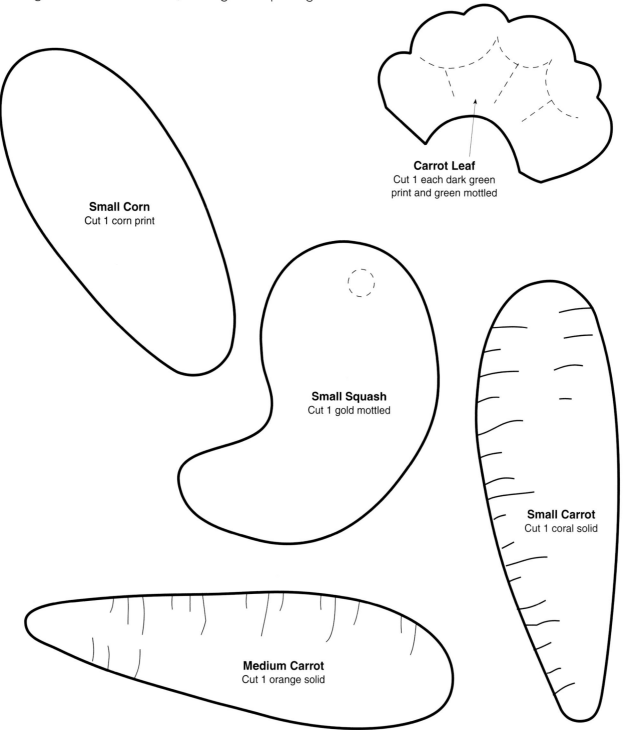

Carrot Leaf
Cut 1 each dark green print and green mottled

Small Corn
Cut 1 corn print

Small Squash
Cut 1 gold mottled

Small Carrot
Cut 1 coral solid

Medium Carrot
Cut 1 orange solid

Framed Poinsettia

Poinsettias are perfect
for any decor.

Block Size
8½" x 8½"

Materials
- 5½" x 5½" square white solid
- 4 strips green print 2" x 5½"
- 4 squares red-and-green plaid 2" x 2"
- Scraps red and green solids, green print and gold lamé
- 1 square each backing and batting 8½" x 8½"
- ⅛ yard medium-weight fusible interfacing
- 1 yard red self-made or purchased binding

Instructions

COLOR KEY
- ▣ Red-and-green plaid
- ▨ Red solid
- ▨ Green solid
- ▨ Green print
- ▨ Gold lamé

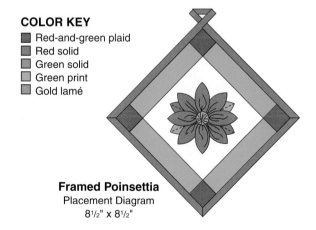

Framed Poinsettia
Placement Diagram
8½" x 8½"

1. Prepare templates for poinsettia petal/leaf and yo-yo pattern pieces given on page 93; cut as directed on pieces.

2. Prepare appliqué pieces for one poinsettia motif with leaves and a gold lamé center yo-yo referring to General Instructions for Appliqué on page 82. **Note:** *For poinsettias, leave bottom edges open. For poinsettia petals, hand-sew a gathering stitch*

at the bottom raw edge; gather tightly and knot to hold. Sew eight petal pieces together at center gathers to make a circle to turn flower.

3. Appliqué the poinsettia motif to the 5½" x 5½" white solid square referring to General Instructions for Appliqué.

4. Sew a 2" x 5½" strip green print to opposite sides of the appliquéd center; press seams toward strips. Sew a 2" x 2" red-and-green plaid square to each end of the two remaining strips. Sew a strip to each remaining side; press seams toward strips.

5. Sandwich batting square between appliquéd square and backing square; pin or baste layers together to hold flat.

6. Quilt center design as desired.

7. Bind edges with red self-made or purchased binding, making a loop on one corner with binding when stitching as shown in Figure 1. ■

Figure 1
Make loop on 1 corner
when binding.

Dresden Plate Poinsettia

This pot holder makes a pretty hostess gift.

Block Size
Approximately 10" in diameter

Materials
- 1 square each 7" x 7" and 11" x 11" white solid
- Scraps red and green solids, red and green prints, red-and-green plaid and gold lamé
- Batting 11" x 11"
- ⅛ yard medium-weight fusible interfacing

Instructions

COLOR KEY
- ■ Red-and-green plaid
- ■ Red print
- ■ Red solid
- □ Green solid
- □ Green print
- □ Gold lamé

Dresden Plate Poinsettia
Placement Diagram
Approximately 10" in diameter

1. Prepare templates for poinsettia petal/leaf and yo-yo pattern pieces; cut as directed on pieces for this project.

2. Prepare appliqué pieces for one poinsettia motif with leaves and a gold lamé center yo-yo referring to General Instructions for Appliqué on page 82. **Note:** *For poinsettias, leave bottom edges open. For poinsettia petals, hand-sew a gathering stitch at the bottom raw edge; gather tightly and knot to hold. Sew eight petal pieces together at center gathers to make a circle to form flower.*

3. Fold 7" x 7" square white solid in quarters; crease. Cut to make circle as shown in Figure 1.

Figure 1
Cut folded square to make circle.

4. Appliqué the poinsettia motif to the 7" x 7" white solid circle referring to General Instructions for Appliqué.

5. Prepare template for A; cut as directed on piece. Join eight A's to make half a circle as shown in Figure 2; repeat for second half circle. Join two halves to make a circle; press seams in one direction.

Figure 2
Join A units to make half a circle.

6. Turn under inside edge of pieced A section ¼"; press. Pin pieced A section to the appliquéd white solid circle at seam line. **Note:** *You may need to adjust placement for the A section to lie flat.* Blind-stitch in place as for poinsettia motif in step 4.

7. Cut a 1¾" x 4" bias strip from a red scrap. Fold under ¼" along each 4" edge; press. Fold in half along length again and stitch close to edge to make a finished strip. Pin both ends to top of one A piece referring to Figure 3; machine-baste to hold in place.

Figure 3
Pin ends of strip to appliquéd piece to make a loop as shown.

8. Pin appliquéd top to the 11" white solid square, right sides together. Pin batting square to the wrong side of the 11" white solid square. Sew all around following edges of A pieces, leaving a 2" opening for turning right side out. Trim excess batting and backing, clip points and trim seams. Turn right side out through opening using a stylet, knitting needle or pencil with broken lead to poke out points and smooth curves. Hand-stitch opening closed.

9. Quilt around motif as desired. ■

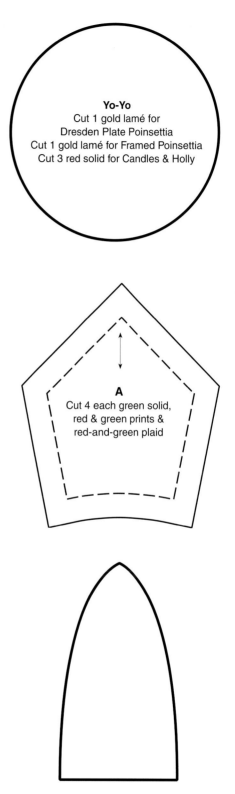

Yo-Yo
Cut 1 gold lamé for
Dresden Plate Poinsettia
Cut 1 gold lamé for Framed Poinsettia
Cut 3 red solid for Candles & Holly

A
Cut 4 each green solid,
red & green prints &
red-and-green plaid

Poinsettia Petal/Leaf
Cut 2 each green solid & green print & 8 red solid
each for Dresden Plate Poinsettia & Framed Poinsettia

Candles & Holly

Decorate your Christmas
table with candles.

Block Size
8½" x 8½"

Materials
- 9" x 9" square red-and-green plaid
- 10" x 10" square white solid
- Scraps red and green solids, green print and gold lamé
- 1 square each backing and batting 8½" x 8½"
- ⅛ yard medium-weight fusible interfacing
- 1 yard red self-made or purchased binding

Instructions

COLOR KEY
■ Red-and-green plaid
■ Red solid
■ Green solid
■ Green print
■ Gold lamé

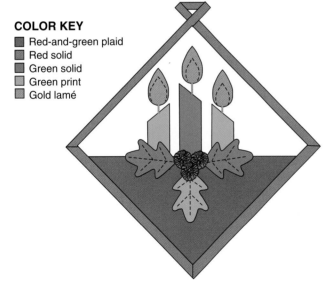

Candles & Holly
Placement Diagram
8½" x 8½"

1. Prepare templates for holly leaves and yo-yos (page 93); cut as directed on each piece. Prepare templates for candle shapes, flame and D and C using patterns given; cut as directed on pieces.

2. Sew C to D as shown in Figure 1 to make pot holder background.

Figure 1
Sew D to C as shown.

3. Make berry yo-yos and prepare pieces for appliqué referring to General Instructions for Appliqué on page 82.

4. Appliqué candle shapes and leaf motifs with berries to the background square referring to the Placement Diagram for positioning and General Instructions for Appliqué on page 82.

5. Sandwich batting square between appliquéd square and backing square; pin or baste layers together to hold flat.

6. Quilt center design as desired.

7. Bind edges with red self-made or purchased binding, making a loop on one corner with binding when stitching as shown in Figure 2. ■

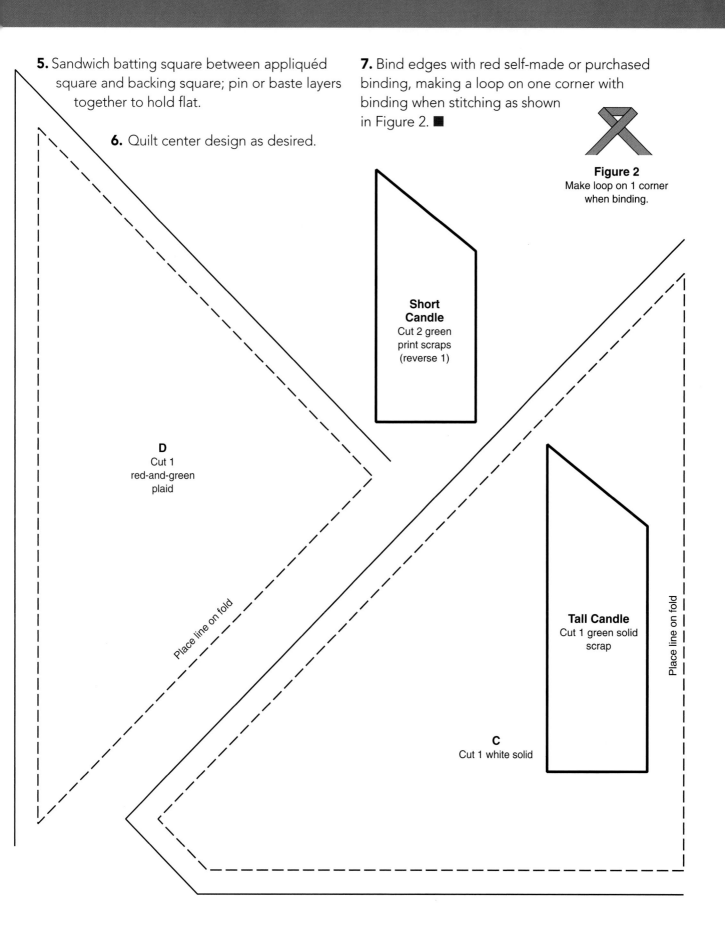

Figure 2
Make loop on 1 corner when binding.

Short Candle
Cut 2 green print scraps (reverse 1)

D
Cut 1 red-and-green plaid

Place line on fold

Tall Candle
Cut 1 green solid scrap

Place line on fold

C
Cut 1 white solid

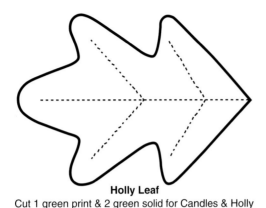

Holly Leaf
Cut 1 green print & 2 green solid for Candles & Holly

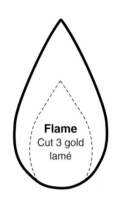

Flame
Cut 3 gold
lamé

Metric Conversion Charts

Metric Conversions

U.S. Measurements		Multiplied by		Metric Measurement
yards	x	.9144	=	meters (m)
yards	x	91.44	=	centimeters (cm)
inches	x	2.54	=	centimeters (cm)
inches	x	25.40	=	millimeters (mm)
inches	x	.0254	=	meters (m)

Metric Measurements		Multiplied by		U.S. Measurements
centimeters	x	.3937	=	inches
meters	x	1.0936	=	yards

Standard Equivalents

U.S. Measurement		Metric Measurement		
1/8 inch	=	3.20 mm	=	0.32 cm
1/4 inch	=	6.35 mm	=	0.635 cm
3/8 inch	=	9.50 mm	=	0.95 cm
1/2 inch	=	12.70 mm	=	1.27 cm
5/8 inch	=	15.90 mm	=	1.59 cm
3/4 inch	=	19.10 mm	=	1.91 cm
7/8 inch	=	22.20 mm	=	2.22 cm
1 inch	=	25.40 mm	=	2.54 cm
1/8 yard	=	11.43 cm	=	0.11 m
1/4 yard	=	22.86 cm	=	0.23 m
3/8 yard	=	34.29 cm	=	0.34 m
1/2 yard	=	45.72 cm	=	0.46 m
5/8 yard	=	57.15 cm	=	0.57 m
3/4 yard	=	68.58 cm	=	0.69 m
7/8 yard	=	80.00 cm	=	0.80 m
1 yard	=	91.44 cm	=	0.91 m

E-mail: Customer_Service@whitebirches.com

HOUSE of WHITE BIRCHES
PUBLISHERS SINCE 1947

100 QUICK-TO-QUILT POT HOLDERS is published by House of White Birches, 306 East Parr Road, Berne, IN 46711, telephone (260) 589-4000. Printed in USA. Copyright © 2004 House of White Birches.

RETAILERS: If you would like to carry this pattern book or any other House of White Birches publications, call the Wholesale Department at Annie's Attic to set up a direct account: (903) 636-4303. Also, request a complete listing of publications available from House of White Birches.

Every effort has been made to ensure that the instructions in this pattern book are complete and accurate. We cannot, however, take responsibility for human error, typographical mistakes or variations in individual work.

ISBN: 1-59217-045-5
4 5 6 7 8 9

Pot Holders on pages 4–36 designed by Ruth Swasey.
Pot Holders on pages 83–96 designed by Barbara Clayton.
We thank Carol Neuenschwander for stitching and Janice Hancock for quilting several of the pot holders.

STAFF

Editor: Jeanne Stauffer
Technical Editor: Sandra L. Hatch
Associate Editor: Dianne Schmidt
Technical Artists: Connie Rand, Chad Summers
Copy Editors: Michelle Beck, Nicki Lehman, Conor Allen
Graphic Arts Supervisor: Ronda Bechinski
Graphic Artist: Glenda Chamberlain
Photography: Tammy Christian, Kelly Heydinger, Christena Green
Photo Stylist: Tammy Nussbaum